ORGANIZING YOUR YOUTH MINISTRY

OTHER YOUTH SPECIALTIES BOOKS

ORGANIZING YOUR YOUTH MINISTRY

PAUL BORTHWICK

Youth Specialties

ZONDERVAN PUBLISHING HOUSE
Grand Rapids, Michigan

ORGANIZING YOUR YOUTH MINISTRY

Youth Specialties books are published by the Zondervan Publishing House
1415 Lake Drive, S.E., Grand Rapids, Michigan 49506

Copyright © 1988 by Youth Specialties, Inc.

Library of Congress Cataloging in Publication Data

Borthwick, Paul, 1954–
  Organizing your youth ministry.

  Bibliography:p.
  1. Church work with youth. I. Title.
BV4447.B68   1988   259'.2   87-29658
ISBN 0-310-44560-4

All Scripture quotations, unless otherwise noted, are taken from the HOLY BIBLE: NEW INTERNATIONAL VERSION (North American Edition). Copyright © 1973, 1978, 1984, by the International Bible Society. Used by permission of Zondervan Bible Publishers.

Chapters 1 and 18 are adapted from articles that appeared in *Group* magazine (and later in *The Youth Leader's Personal Management Handbook*). Chapters 3, 5, 10, 11, 21, and 22 are adapted from articles that appeared in *Youthworker Journal*. Chapters 2 and 17 contain portions that originally appeared in *Leadership*. Chapter 17 is revised from the booklet *How to Plan, Develop, and Lead a Youth Missionary Team* (published by Grace Chapel in 1981).

Edited by Linda Vanderzalm

Printed in the United States of America

  89   90   91   92 / AF / 10   9   8   7   6   5   4   3   2

Contents

Foreword

There is no ministry in the total task of the church more challenging or demanding than that of working with and guiding its youth. Increasingly, churches of every size are sensing the importance of its young people—and crying out for help.

Experienced youth director and pastor, Paul Borthwick, is forcefully answering this cry in a practical, helpful, demonstrable way in this book which comes out of the crucible of labor and learning, success and failure.

Not only does Paul draw from his experience from leadership of a magnetic and eminently successful youth program in a large and effective church, but shows how the principles successfully applied at Grace Chapel in Lexington, Massachusetts, are transferable to other situations, whether small or large, urban or rural, doctrinally diverse. It is eminently helpful for both professional and volunteer youth workers.

The book is well-titled, for author Borthwick comes back repeatedly to his theme of *organization* which forms the basis for effectiveness in ministry. Biblical principles are carefully and accurately applied and the up-beat practicability of the wholesome methodology is demonstrated throughout. And it is fascinating reading, without a dry or dull page throughout.

Every youth director, youth leader, counselor, pastor guiding a youth staff, concerned parents will find so much by way of both helpful encouragement and mature insights in ministering to youth, who obviously represent the future of any church and community.

Paul Borthwick's focus is right on target as he addresses

himself to the leader's personal agenda and responsibility, then moves into action in leading both his team and the youth as they face the day-to-day, rubber-meeting-the-road challenges which are inescapable for the Youth Director. This is not mere philosophy— it is workable, practical counsel and direction coming out of a decade or more of failure and gain, spiritual "profit and loss."

An added value to this material is the most helpful resource suggestions which are offered at the conclusion of each major section.

I have a sense that this book will soon become "must" reading for every conscientious leader of our treasured youth and could well become a text book for those whom God is calling into this high and holy ministry among our precious young men women.

How I wish, decades ago as I was in an international youth ministry, as well as active on a local scene, I could have had the advantage of this sage and Godly advice. Where were you, Paul, when I needed you?

The ministry among the youth of our churches is going to be measurably advanced as the clearly enunciated, biblical principles shared in this book are put to work under the leadership of the Holy Spirit through those special servants of God called to lead our beautiful young people to become "complete in Christ" (Colossians 1:28).

Ted W. Engstrom
President
World Vision

Preface

Dozens of people have contributed, directly or indirectly, to the writing of this book. I am grateful to the people who worked with me, inspired me, and encouraged me to make this book a reality.

Special thanks are due to Grace Chapel's youth staff and youth ministry interns, who over the years have made me see the need for better administration, training, and leadership in our youth ministry. Of these, Dan Mahoney, Tom McLaughlin, Tim Conder, and Betty Stanbery have given invaluable assistance.

Betty Stanbery and Jeff Collins deserve special thanks as they forced me to think more about Sunday school and youth music respectively. Chapters 12 and 16 reflect many ideas they taught me.

Steve Macchia has served as a constant encouragement to me as my boss and partner in ministry. Dianne Stephens and Cathy Franzoni also have been great encouragers in my writing and have painstakingly typed the manuscript for this book.

Beyond the people at Grace Chapel, I am deeply indebted to my youth ministry partners who have discipled me, taught me about planning and directing programs, and helped me develop a good sense of professionalism in youth ministry. Most outstanding in this category are John Musselman, Noel Becchetti, Duffy Robbins, Jack Gerry, Brent Bromstrup, Dave Busby, and Jim Burns.

Finally, I am thankful for my precious wife, Christie. She has been my faithful partner in ministry since 1978 and has taught me about balancing administration with meeting people's needs. If it were not for her insight, I think that I would have been tempted to think that programs were an end in themselves.

Recognizing how much she has taught me and how much she has sacrificed to let me lead our youth ministry and to write this book, I dedicate this book to her.

Paul Borthwick

Introduction:
The Need To Organize

Someday I'll submit a cartoon to a magazine for youth leaders. The first frame will show me alone in my office, reviewing the youth ministry schedule, the address list, and the goal sheet; the caption will read: "How can I ever do it?" The second frame will show me reviewing the monthly calendar with my wife, who looks at me with an expression of frustration; the caption will read: "When are you going to stop?" The third frame will show the church leaders looking over a copy of the youth schedule; the caption will read: "What exactly *do* you do?"

The tensions of youth ministry are summed up in these cartoons: the demands we put on ourselves, the need to balance our personal lives with ministry, and other people's expectations all operate as powerful tentacles that pull us in different directions. How can we find balance?

Looking at the multiple responsibilities related to youth groups—the various programs for junior high students, senior high students, and, at times, the college-age ministry along with the administrative workload related to budgets, meetings, mailings, preparation for talks, and training sessions—can be overwhelming.

THREE PROBLEMS

This sense of being overwhelmed usually results from three basic problems that youth leaders often have:

Problem #1: We have too much to do in too little time.

Problem #2: We have difficulty choosing our priorities in the face of the many responsibilities we feel.

Problem #3: What *should* be done first isn't always what we *want* to do first.

These three problems combine with multiple demands and expectations to form one distinct cry: we need to get organized! We need to organize others to help us so that we don't it all alone. We need to regain a sense of personal growth and family life so that our lives are more properly balanced. We need to learn to account for our time and our priorities so that we can answer board members who ask us what we do with our time. We need to get organized so that we can direct our energies to the most important tasks—even when these might not be what we would like to do.

This book is designed to help youth workers organize five different areas:

1. Personal. Many of us entered youth ministry with great dreams but with no idea of how to realize them. We plunged into our work, giving 110 percent to the youth ministry. But then "real life" hit—spouses, children, homes, checking accounts, retirement plans, and education. Now we must work to balance all these important elements that demand our energy and attention. If we are to have an effective youth ministry, we must work toward individual growth, a healthy personal life, good relationships, and positive self-esteem. Too many of us look at these things as potential *results* of good ministry, but the reverse is usually true: good ministry is a result of a balanced personal life.

2. Professional. Whether we want to admit it or not, our ability to be organized and to administer our youth ministries will influence how others view the profession of youth ministry. In the Christian world, where youth ministry is sometimes seen as a stepping-stone to "real, adult ministry" and other times as a ministry for those who refuse to grow up, we are the ones who will help other people see youth ministry either as a worthy profession or just a fun-and-games operation.

3. Ministry. We have been called to serve people. Yet we sometimes find ourselves spending inordinate amounts of time doing things that don't relate to our primary purpose of caring for people. There are no shortcut remedies to such a problem, but better planning and time management can create programs, lessons, and activities that help people grow, learn, and love each other.

4. Vision. Getting organized will free us to gain vision for ourselves and our ministries. Planning, goal setting, and long-term thinking is needed for those of us who sometimes live as spontaneously as the teenagers we disciple. We need to organize so that we can look beyond the next program and upcoming retreat to see where all our efforts are leading.

5. Obedience. Ephesians 5, verse 16 tells us to "make the most of the time because the days are evil." Such teaching is challenging to youth workers, who are privileged to work with students at the most formative years of their lives. Yet time is short. In their adolescent years, students will make some of the most important decisions of their lives, decisions that will affect them for years to come. This sense of urgency calls us to better organization. If we are to be obedient to the Scriptures, we must work hard to plan and to lead our ministries.

MORE EFFECTIVE MINISTRY

This book won't solve all your youth ministry problems, but it will raise questions and offer answers that should help increase your effectiveness as a youth minister.

To help us focus on the various issues in youth ministry, this book is divided into four sections. Part I, the most personal, addresses issues related to our own lives, families, and personal growth. Part II addresses philosophical foundations to youth ministry programming and planning, helping us ask why we do what we do. Part III covers the daily, weekly, monthly, and yearly administrative demands of the youth ministry, from budgets to retreats, from activities to Sunday school lessons. Part IV helps us evaluate our goals and methods.

We do need to get organized, both personally and professionally, but the ultimate purpose isn't just to produce better programs or a more efficient discipleship system. The ultimate purpose is to present each person "complete in Christ" (Col. 1:28 NASB). I hope these chapters encourage each of you to organize your youth ministry toward that end.

Part I

GETTING ORGANIZED

In the early days of attending conferences, workshops, and seminars on youth ministry, I would go with eyes wide open, eager to find the "guaranteed solutions" to my ministry or personal problems. After a powerful message by one of the experts, I would say to myself, "Yes! That's just what I need. I'm going to implement that idea right away!"

But then I had to return home—to the youth group, our church, my daily routines—and all of my great intentions would come to naught. Later, I would resist reading over my journal for fear of finding an entry in which I had made bold claims or promises about my life or ministry. In short, I had a tough time reconciling the dreams that I had for my life and ministry with the realities of my daily living and my leadership.

At times I would be tempted to rationalize, "If only I had *his* church situation," or "If I had a budget like hers, I could build a ministry like that too." My excuses were futile. I finally had to admit that there was no perfect environment, no perfect ministry, no perfect solution to issues that required discipline and involved people. I finally had to realize that getting organized, finding the solutions to my ministry struggles, and getting a better grip on the multiple responsibilities I was facing *started with me*. Good leadership and good organization ultimately started with me.

Why are our own lives an important place to start?

. . . because the way we see ourselves and our own lives will ultimately work itself into the way we view our youth ministries. We who are frequently telling students why they should have positive self-esteem need to think about our own self-image.

. . . because our personal growth as adults, family members, and professionals will ultimately affect the growth of our family members, our co-workers, and the students themselves. If we want to have a youth leadership team and a youth ministry that is growing, we must be growing ourselves.

. . . because good personal management and organization can create a healthier environment for us and can help us to endure in youth ministry. If we are skilled in time and people management, we can reverse the negative trend toward high turnover that harms many youth groups.

. . . because our personal priorities and our deepest personal commitments will reveal themselves in our ministries. If we are committed to excellence or obedience or loyalty, the youth ministry will reflect this.

. . . because organization will help us temper our expectations, determine our ministry purpose, and give us a realistic overview of what we will be able to accomplish.

Although it may seem artificial to separate ourselves from our programs, we need to understand how our personalities, temperaments, and emotions affect the ministries we lead. Part I will examine this in some detail.

1.
HOW DO YOU VIEW YOURSELF?

Youth minister Terry is forty-one years old, but he tries to look younger. He uses teenage slang, and his jokes are modeled after those he hears at the high schools he visits. Some people actually think Terry is in his early twenties, except for his receding hairline and large belly.

Joan is twenty-five, so looking and feeling young isn't a problem. She hangs around with her youth group members at the pizza house on Saturday nights. She goes to all the high school athletic events, and she volunteers to chaperone dances. She has few friends her own age.

Rob has adult friends, and he looks adult, but he acts like the junior high students with whom he works. He often embarrasses his wife with his behavior in public. Leaders of the church often ask themselves, "Will Rob ever grow up?"

The issue in these people's ministries is a weak self-concept, brought on by an intense desire to be accepted by the teenagers with whom they work. Having a poor self-image is a problem we all face at one time or another in our ministry with youth. How do we feel secure enough to be ourselves? How do we build the confidence needed to be stable in our own self-images?

WHY SELF-DOUBT?

We often doubt ourselves because of our inability to handle three issues:

Age. The issue of age is a no-win situation in youth work. If we are young, parents and other adults often think of us as immature and unwise; we doubt our own effectiveness with youth when someone asks why we don't have *adults* involved with the youth group. On the other hand, those of us who are older often feel ill-equipped to work with youth because we feel out of touch. When we get the invitation to our tenth or twentieth high school reunion, many of us wonder if we're fooling ourselves about being effective with youth. When we haven't resolved the issue of age in our lives, we either resort to bizarre behavior (such as Terry or Rob) or we resign, thinking we can no longer be useful.

Performance. What is "success" in youth ministry? Is it having a large group or a large, flashy retreat? Is success giving the students a good time every week?

We struggle within ourselves to be important. We know that long-term commitment to youth work is a key to effectiveness, but we wonder whether that commitment will satisfy our need for personal success. Then we compare ourselves with our peers: "What am I doing in youth work? My friends are lawyers, business executives, and doctors; I work with teenagers. Other volunteers in the church are leading our congregation in great decisions; I scarcely can lead a junior high Christmas party."

Results. "Why haven't you changed my kid yet?" It's amazing, isn't it, how some parents who have failed to communicate with their children in fifteen years expect us to make miraculous changes in fifteen weeks. Yet our inability to perform miracles gnaws at us, and we question our effectiveness, our abilities, and our calling. We may want to quit. We might try to blame others. We might even ask God why he allows us to be so fruitless. All these thoughts lead us to the desperate conclusion: I'm worthless. I'm a failure.

BUILD A POSITIVE SELF-IMAGE

Struggles with our self-image are inevitable, but we can take certain steps to protect our weak spirits and to strengthen our ability to see ourselves as God sees us.

Find a sounding board. In my earliest years of youth ministry, Norman never tired of hearing my complaints and fears about youth ministry. When I wondered if it was all worth it, he'd help me see God's perspective both of me and my work.

My wife, Christie, is now my sounding board. She listens and responds without criticism, but she loves me enough to offer her acceptance, well-timed rebukes, and affirmation.

Without such friends, I doubt if I could have stayed in youth ministry. They have been God's messengers, sent to help me recognize the good he is doing in and through me. They also have prodded me when I have been tempted to wallow in self-pity. Their words have strengthened my ability to understand how God sees me.

Develop outside interests. Youth work can devour all our time. Without exercising caution, we can find ourselves at the end of each week with no time for rest or rejuvenation.

Having a healthy self-image requires that we have some interests outside the youth group. We need to pursue interests in sports, the arts, music, or special hobbies so we can be deeper and broader people. Someone may respond, "But I can't see how going to the opera will make a better youth leader." But being a great youth leader isn't the only reason for living. Outside interests can help us grow in our perspective of life and can deliver us from the nearsightedness that says the youth group is all that matters.

Allow for depression. Some days our self-doubt, negative feelings, and sense of worthlessness are overwhelming. The down time may come in the middle of winter or after someone criticizes our ministry. Depression may strike even after a successful youth event.

Knowing ourselves and being honest about these down times is the first place to start. During these times, we may need to retreat to cultivate our relationship with God. We may need the counsel of our sounding-board person. Or like Elijah in 1 Kings 19, we may just need a meal and a good night's sleep.

While we shouldn't indulge ourselves with self-pity, we have to allow for the times when our feelings are low. God can speak to us in these times, but this will happen only when we realize that it's OK to come to him in the midst of our fears and insecurities.

Visit other groups. Visiting other groups can show us where we are succeeding, where we need to grow. But above all, it can reassure us that we aren't alone. When discouraged youth leaders visit our youth group, they sometimes ask: "Do you mean that you have problems with cliques too? You have problems getting group members to sing? Your group feels bored and apathetic sometimes too?" They probably thought their groups' problems were unique. They probably felt like isolated failures, until they realized their struggles were typical.

Develop a team. We need the body of Christ to realize a sense of personal worth and to grow in our ability to accept ourselves. We need a youth ministry team, a group of co-workers who share the leadership load.

A youth leadership team characterized by love, honesty, and sensitivity can enable every team member to maximize his or her gifts and abilities. The team can free up the older members to be the respected sages and the younger members to be their enthusiastic selves. The team can protect us from criticism and provide the strength we need when endurance is waning.

A twenty-one-year-old member of our youth ministry team was recently faulted by parents for being immature and irresponsible. Devastated by the criticism, Jack wanted to quit the team. Through the team's support, he changed his mind. The team helped him to see through the parents' criticism to the struggles those parents were having with their teenagers. With honest love the team encouraged Jack to face his immaturity and to become more responsible than he had been.

Nurture your relationship to God. To base how we feel about ourselves on things that shift and change (like success or others' opinions of us) is asking for trouble. We need a solid foundation on which to build our view of ourselves. That foundation is God.

When we maintain our relationship to God as top priority, we find that God's opinion of us matters more than others' criticism. When we feel inadequate because of our age, God can comfort us. When performance pressures mount, we can remember that God sees accomplishments that others can't see. When lack of results bogs us down, we can remember that God asks us to be faithful, not successful.

Through our relationship to God, our partnership with others, and our own personal growth, we can develop peace and confidence in ourselves and in the work to which God has directed us.

2.
MANAGING YOURSELF

The youth group at Edgewood Baptist Church is barely surviving. After Jim's departure (the third leader in four years), most of the young people are pessimistic. Some, with their families, have started attending the United Methodist church because of its solid youth ministry. Other teenagers have abandoned any aspirations of Christian growth, and they rarely come to church.

Jim had come in the fall with high hopes and long-term commitment. Some of the students believed him when he talked about "going with you through high school," but others were skeptical. His two predecessors had said something similar.

Jim had intended to stay a long time, but discouragement, a few failures, and a better opportunity caused him to give his departure notice in April. Adults were surprised and disappointed; the teenagers shrugged their shoulders as if to say, "Who's next?"

WHY THE TURNOVER?

One denomination admits that its youth ministers change every seven months. Other reports are not so grim, but the general consensus is that the average tenure of a youth minister isn't more than eighteen months.

Veteran youth leaders claim it takes up to two years to reach teenagers effectively. So many men and women are leaving youth ministries before effectiveness begins. Why are they leaving?

"God directed me elsewhere." Many youth workers are in their early twenties, so marriage, children, or schooling can draw them

away from youth ministry. Others feel led to go elsewhere, but this often camouflages the fact that from the beginning they viewed youth ministry as a stepping stone to other things. When a pastorate or another church responsibility appeared, they abandoned the youth ministry.

"The church drove me out." Sometimes churches demand too much. When a fellow youth pastor told me that he was quitting because he had been working ninety hours per week with junior high students, I affirmed his decision.

A more subtle push comes when people treat the youth minister as a junior minister or as a big adolescent. When a well-meaning parent asks, "Do you need any *adults* to go on the retreat?" or a deacon says, "So when are you going to be a *real* minister?" youth pastors know they are in the minor leagues. They may leave in an effort to appear more mature.

"I just couldn't do it." Some people legitimately recognize their inability to work with teenagers and get out of youth ministry. Unfortunately though, many quit because they place excessive demands on themselves. They expect too much, and when they fail, they assume it is God's way of telling them to bail out.

No matter what reasons are given for a youth minister's leaving, the results are the same: students get frustrated and even hostile. They feel rejected; they are told in one more way that they are not important. The departure of one leader sometimes guarantees the failure of the next. Teens who have seen several turnovers often approach a new person with an attitude that says, "Let's see how long it takes to get rid of this one."

In my opinion, however, many people prematurely leave the youth ministry because of poor personal management. I believe that youth workers can take steps to strengthen their personal management and to endure in youth ministry. I offer these suggestions to improving personal management, family management, and ministry management.

PERSONAL MANAGEMENT

1. *Study.* If asked what they have been reading lately, many youth ministers hesitate. With the exception of "Twenty New

Retreat Ideas," many youth ministers rarely read. The irony is that most of us have college/seminary degrees. We know effective ministry requires effective study, but we sometimes affirm the opposite.

To get back into the study habit, consider these steps:

- Block off study time on your schedule.

- Ask yourself weekly, "What am I reading that's not related to youth ministry?"

- Buy a challenging book to read and discuss with your spouse or close friend.

- Research a youth ministry project.

Study builds awareness that youth ministry is a profession to be pursued rather than a trial to be endured until someone offers a new job. Study also builds expertise about youth ministry issues. Most important, it often helps to deepen our personal spirituality.

2. *Set personal and ministry goals.* Too few youth ministers are asking themselves where they will be in three or five years. We are often too busy developing a "bag of tricks" to increase attendance and stimulate involvement. But when the bag of tricks is exhausted, so are we.

We must learn to think about our future. Very few people became youth ministers haphazardly. Most, upon personal reflection and self-examination before God, sensed a call to youth ministry over a long term. We must also think long term about ministry goals. When our church administrator asks what my four-year plan is for discipling high schoolers, I am challenged to look at the ministry as a process, not just a yearly program.

3. *Grow beyond your ministry.* Involve yourself in some area besides youth ministry. Offer to preach or administer communion or counsel an older person.

One church practices a "major-minor" concept. To prevent stagnation, the church encourages its ministers to have a "major" (principle field of ministry) and a "minor" (a small responsibility in an unrelated field). A musical youth minister could direct the choir one week while the music minister taught youth Sunday school.

This added experience allows us to grow in new areas, providing stimulation and sending us back to the youth group refreshed. I have been stimulated by the opportunity to lead youth mission teams. These experiences have stretched me administratively, spiritually, and emotionally. In many respects they are a reward to me as well as a benefit to our church. The church, by allowing me to go on these projects, gets me back refreshed and invigorated for another year of ministry.

4. *Grow outside your ministry.* Find people and activities that will stimulate you. I find fresh insights and new resources from the youth ministers (especially the long-term ones) whom I have met at conferences and workshops. This fellowship with others in youth ministry has often defused my Elijah complex ("I, only I am left"). Setting aside the money to attend these workshops yields far more than just a new youth program.

Another opportunity that can revitalize us in youth ministry is outside speaking engagements. When we visit other youth groups, we will usually realize two things: that we are doing better than we thought we were and that we communicate more effectively than we realized we did. When we visit other youth groups, we often see the same flaws that are in our group. Furthermore, the new audience may appreciate us ten times more than our group, and it reassures us that God is using us.

Ridge Burns, a veteran youth minister now working in California, adds another dimension:

> I know that there are many youth workers experiencing burnout. I think that youth workers would not burn out if they would plan their lives with some alternative interests. My wife and I take a three-month sabbatical in missions every four years. Whatever the endeavor, youth workers need to plan their lives so that they are growing. This is the only way that we can stay on the cutting edge of working with high schoolers for long periods, or even for our lives.[1]

FAMILY MANAGEMENT

1. *Guard your personal life.* If you are a single youth worker, you must work hard to grow outside of relationships with

---

[1] Ridge Burns, (interview with), *Youthletter*, Evangelical Ministries (Mar. 1982), 23.

teenagers. Effective youth ministers sometimes can spend so much time with teenagers that they forget how twenty-two year olds or thirty year olds act. You need to have peer fellowship and to grow as adults.

Married youth workers need quality time with their spouses and family. One girl told me that the youth minister at her former church had "open campus" at his house six nights a week so that teenagers could drop by any time. When I first heard this, I was full of guilt for my selfishness (I protected three nights per week). But when I learned that this man's marriage was in disrepair and that he had left the ministry, I reconfirmed my decision to be protective. We must recognize our families as God-given priorities. (The "Diary of a Mad Housewife" at the end of this chapter is a stinging rebuke to all of us who have ever gotten our priorities confused.)

2. *Take time off.* Time away from our work refreshes us and makes us able to function more effectively.

> A legend of John the Evangelist tells us that John was once playing with a partridge. Someone chided him for resting and enjoying the partridge in play rather than being busy at work. John answered, "I see you carry a bow. Why is it that you don't have it strung and ready for use?" He was told, "That would not do at all. If I kept it strung and ready for use, it would be lax and be good for nothing." "Then," said John, "don't wonder about what I'm doing."[2]

We often approach our lives and ministries "strung too tight." While at a youth workers' conference, I skipped a main session to confer with a youth ministry professor. As we talked in the hotel lobby, my three youth ministry interns walked by, wearing swimsuits and toting towels; they were obviously headed for the pool. Wanting to impress the youth ministry professor, I told the interns I was embarrassed to see them skip the meeting. We talked, and they told me of the overload they were experiencing due to seminars, sessions, and lectures. Then one of the interns summed it all up: "You can't get burned out by what you burn off."

Perhaps we all need to learn how to burn off some energy and stress so that we and our families can relax.

---

[2] Wayne Oates, *Confessions of a Workaholic*, (Nashville, TN: Abdington Press, 1971), 24.

MINISTRY MANAGEMENT

Although many of these principles will be referred to later in the book, they deserve mention here because they relate to the overall sense of personal management.

1. *Affirm the call to youth ministry.* Although we undoubtedly will have days when we will want to throw in the towel, we must remember to affirm regularly God's calling us to youth ministry. The word *calling*, however, implies a long, perhaps even a lifelong, commitment.

I have been challenged by veteran youth workers who have called for (and exemplified) a serious calling to youth ministry. Dean Borgman, professor at Gordon-Conwell Theological Seminary, wants the church to see "youth work as a *professional,* ordainable ministry rather than just a stepping-stone to the pastorate." Dawson McAllister, national youth speaker and writer, urges churches to find "youth workers who are committed to staying in one place for more than a year. This is the only way to communicate love effectively and build the trust that teens need."

The underlying philosophy here is that teenagers respond best to relationships that are stable and trustworthy. Teenagers take a long time to open up to older people. So as we contemplate a call to youth ministry, we must think in terms of three or more years as the minimum.

We must reaffirm that youth ministry is a profession, a ministry, and a calling. It isn't merely something to do to pass the time while waiting for a "real" job after college or seminary. As we affirm it as a calling, we can take the entire idea of managing youth ministry more seriously.

2. *Be a part of the church staff team.* In Craig's church, he is viewed as a baby-sitter whose expertise is directing teenagers through adolescence. He has few responsibilities outside the youth group, and he never participates in planning or priority setting for the church. No wonder he feels as if he works on a lonely island; no wonder he wants to quit.

At Grace Chapel, I have been allowed to participate in planning, in worship services, and in brainstorming for the future. I am a full member of the church staff, and the youth ministry is

27

constantly exhorted to be an integrated part of our church family. I love to work here. I'm free to realize my part in the church team. I carry that positive attitude back to the young people, and I get them excited about being part of the church.

To work on the staff team, however, requires that we demonstrate a commitment to the overall church ministry (not just to our own little kingdom) and that we stay away from the self-pity that sometimes alienates youth workers from other pastoral staff members.

3. *Work through a team.* It's discouraging to lead a youth ministry alone. Many of us aren't the handsome-musical-athletic type. Those who are often get disheartened because they become entertainers rather than ministers.

We must encourage others to help us build a youth ministry team by:

a. *Funneling volunteers our way.* Lay volunteers not only relieve the pressure of a one-person show, but they also enrich the ministry by bringing to the students a diversity of spiritual gifts. Shaping a team of volunteers also fulfills the scriptural call to "equip the saints" to do the ministry.

b. *Pointing out students with leadership abilities.* Competent student leadership helps us keep our role in perspective and helps the students claim greater ownership of the youth group. Youth groups often grow both in size and in spiritual depth when the students themselves assume some leadership functions.

c. *Helping us delegate.* Too many youth workers have burned out because they refused to delegate. (I have often mused about a youth minister's tombstone with the inscription: "He gave his group his all . . . and they took it.") The most successful youth leaders are those who concentrate on their strengths and delegate the rest. When they get a new idea, they initiate it and train someone else to execute it.

A friend and I both have long-standing youth ministries built on this team concept. For him, it has been hard because he has multiple talents and could do everything better by leading it himself. He is musical, athletic, humorous, and an excellent teacher. Nevertheless he has built a team-led youth ministry because he knows it keeps him from burnout and it reaches a broad diversity of students. I, on the other hand, had no choice. With no musical ability and no desire for fun-and-games leadership, I had to find people to make up for my weaknesses. I try to concentrate on what I do best, and the rest I give to people who are far more talented than I.

DIARY OF A MAD HOUSEWIFE

(A Case Study in Poor Personal and Ministry Management)

My husband is a full-time youth director. He is extremely dedicated and spends between 50 and 70 hours a week with young people. I think the reason he is so successful with kids is that he is always available to them, always ready to help when they need him.

That may be why the attendance has more than doubled in the past year. He really knows how to talk their language. This past year he would be out two and three nights a week talking with kids till midnight. He's always taking them to camps and ski trips and overnight camp-outs. If he isn't with kids, he's thinking about them and preparing for his next encounter with them.

And if he has any time left after that, he is speaking or attending a conference where he can share with others what God is doing through him. When it comes to youth work, my husband has always been 100 percent.

I guess that's why I left him.

There isn't much left after 100 percent. Frankly, I just could not compete with "God." I say that because my husband always had a way of reminding me that this was God's work, and he must minister where and when God called him. Young people today desperately need help and God had called him to help them. When a young person needed him, he had to respond or he would be letting God and the young person down.

When I *did* ask my husband to spend some time with the

kids or me, it was always tentative and if I became pushy about it I was "nagging," "trying to get him out of God's work," "behaving selfishly," or I was revealing a "spiritual problem."

Honestly, I have never wanted anything but God's will for my husband, but I never could get him to consider that maybe his family was part of that will.

It didn't matter how many "discussions" we had about his schedule, he would always end with, "OK, I'll get out of the ministry, if that's what you want." Of course, I didn't want that, so we would continue as always until another "discussion."

You can ask for only so long. There is a limit to how long you can be ignored and put off. You threaten to leave without meaning it till you keep the threat. You consider all the unpleasant consequences till they don't seem unpleasant anymore. You decide that nothing could be more unpleasant than being alone, feeling worthless.

You finally make up your mind that you are a person with real worth as an individual. You assert your ego and join womanhood again. That's what I did. I wanted to be more than housekeeper, diaper changer, and sex partner.

I wanted to be free from the deep bitterness and guilt that slowly ate at my spiritual and psychological sanity. Deep inside there was something making me not only dislike my husband, but everything he did or touched.

His "I love you" became meaningless to me because he didn't act like it. His gifts were evidence to me of his *guilt* because he didn't spend more time with me. His sexual advances were met with a frigidity that frustrated both of us and deepened the gap between us.

All I wanted was to feel as though he really wanted to be with me. But, no matter how hard I tried, I always felt like I was keeping him from something. He had a way of making me feel guilty because I had forced him to spend his valuable time with the kids and me. Just once I wish he would have canceled something for us instead of canceling us.

You don't have to believe this, but I really loved him and his ministry once. I never wanted him to work an eight-to-five job. Nor did I expect him to be home every night. I tried to believe every promise he made me, honestly hoping things would change, but they never did.

All of a sudden I woke up one day and realized that I had become a terribly bitter person. I not only resented my husband and his work, but I was beginning to despise myself. In desperation to save myself, our children and, I guess, even my husband and his ministry, I left him.

I don't think he really believed I'd leave him. I guess I never really believed I'd leave him either.

But I did!

("Diary of a Mad Housewife," by Mike Yaconelli. *The Wittenburg Door*, June, 1971, p. 8.)

3.
MANAGING YOUR MINISTRY

The first call of the day came from one of our church elders. "Hi, Paul; what are you doing today?"

"I'm going to spend the day at two of our high schools."

"Oh, you have some appointments?"

"No," I said. "I try to go to the high schools once a week just to hang around the cafeteria and meet kids."

"Hang around?" he snickered. "Do you think you could find some time this week to squeeze me into your 'busy' schedule?" (A few more laughs.)

Time. Priorities. Planning. Decision making. Although few of us in youth work are called "executives" by the people of our congregations, in one way or another we're making executive decisions all the time: How will we use our time? Where will we devote energies? How can we plan for an effective year?

The tension of this executive posture often results (as it did in my case) from people failing to understand just what is involved in working with youth. We try to explain what we do, but the day-to-day details of youth ministry may be hard to explain.

QUANTIFYING "PEOPLE WORK"

What do we do? Perhaps there is no more disarming question for those in professional ministry. It causes us great discomfort, especially if our use of time is hard to account for or if it isn't in line with the priorities of the person inquiring. Such a question can plunge us into self-doubt and even despair, causing us to question our value to God and to others.

The difficulty with people work like youth ministry is that is can be hard to quantify. We can't measure our accomplishments each week. The visible results of our work with students may surface only over a long period of time.

Perhaps it's hard even for *us* to know what we do. Our schedules are often open-ended, with few measurable deadlines. An open schedule can be both a blessing and a curse. It's a blessing because it frees us to set personal goals, see people, dream, think, and study. But it can also be a curse, leading us into several traps: *overwork* (because we're never quite sure when the job is done); *laziness* (because we don't know what is expected of us); *mismanagement of time* (preparing twenty-five hours for a ten-minute devotional); *crisis orientation* (we sit and wait for a crisis to occur so that we can run to "put out the fire"); or *aimlessness* (we're busy, but our busyness has no aim or focus).

FIVE AREAS OF MANAGEMENT

How do we begin to develop administrative skills? Let's start by identifying five specific managerial challenges we face in youth work. As we see these administrative aspects of our lives and ministries more clearly, we can focus on how to manage them better.

Time management. The proper use of our time is probably the most important management skill we must master as we work with schedules, meetings, appointments, deadlines, and planning. We'd all like more time, but the reality is that we need to make better use of the time we have. We must learn to *account* for our time. The key question here is, *"Do I know where my time is going and why?"*

Personal management. We've already discussed the need to organize and examine our personal lives. We've determined that we need to keep our lives in balance, taking time to grow in areas and with people completely separate from our youth ministries. Sometimes problems that appear to be related to our job skills are really problems in our personal lives. Organizing our job alone will not solve these deep-seated personal questions. As we improve the management of our personal lives, the key question is, *"Am I growing as a Christian and as a person?"*

People management. Youth ministry can be consumed by time spent with people. Crises, counseling appointments, time with parents, students who just need a friend, and discipling relationships all scream for our attention. If left unchecked, they can squeeze the life out of us and our ministries. For that reason, managing people in our ministries means carefully balancing our people time with the time needed for other legitimate priorities.

Managing people also means being able to say no. Our need to be needed often leads us to take people's pursuit of us as an expression of our importance to them (and even to God). When we say yes to everyone, however, we soon find our schedules unbalanced, and our goals and priorities are no longer our own. We begin to live only to fulfill the expectations of others. Improving our people management skills means struggling with this question: *"Am I balancing time with people with my other personal and ministry priorities?"*

Program management. "We care for *people* here. We don't just run a program!" Sound familiar? Perhaps we've even said it ourselves. The paradox here, of course, is that some of our best vehicles for caring for people are well-managed, quality programs.

We in youth leadership tend to make three errors in judgment when we try to manage our programs. The first error is *underestimating the time needed* to plan our programs. A myriad of details take time: buying supplies, making phone calls, delegating responsibilities, training students, planning budgets. When we underestimate that time, the result is frantic, last-minute planning and poorly run programs.

The second error is our *failure to delegate.* Many "secondary" details are involved in the execution of any program, and we should delegate these details to adult volunteers or responsible student helpers.

The third error we make in program management is our *failure to think through our long-term goals.* We fill our youth program schedule just to have something to do. Such planning may alleviate our short-term need for a program, but it seldom leads to youth groups with direction and long-term purpose.

The key question that we must ask ourselves here is this: *"Am I planning my program in light of the time I have to run the program, the people resources available, and the long-term goals of my youth ministry?"*

Environmental management. I am not referring here to pollution or whales, but rather to the management of our work environments. We sometimes work against ourselves in the way we manage our surroundings. We open our letters and scatter them helter-skelter on our desks. We save every publication ever produced just in case we can use them someday. We stack up a pile of "To Read" books. We surround ourselves with posters, pictures, and souvenirs of the youth group. And then, after building our mountains of clutter, we wonder why it's so hard to study. We wonder why we're distracted when we try to think and plan.

The problem is further complicated by the presence of telephones, other workers (in the case of shared offices), or clutter not of our own making (youth "offices" are often the places where churches store athletic equipment, Sunday school materials, and the fifteen-foot gutters used to build mile-long sundaes).

The environments available to us will vary according to our church organization. Some of us will have offices; others of us will have to work at home. Though we can't control all the aspects of our work environments, we can become more effective by asking this key question: *"How can I create a working environment that increases my effectiveness in planning, thinking, and studying?"*

PRACTICAL TIPS FOR BETTER MANAGEMENT

The following ten suggestions cover a broad spectrum of management skills designed to help us identify a few areas to start working toward better management.

1. *Account for your time.* Keep a record of each meeting, each planning session, every hour of study time, every hour spent with students, every hour spent in time with your spouse, etc. Keep

track of how you're using your time over a month. Finding out where our time goes is the first step to improving its management.

2. *Plan your time offensively.* Buy a time-planner or calendar that *works for you.* Then look ahead to the next weeks and months and pencil in your commitments, giving yourself family time, devotional time, and some of the other blocks of time that so easily get pushed out of your schedule. As one management expert put it, "If *you* don't plan your time, someone else will plan it for you." People and responsibilities will always crowd in on our schedules, so our time should be prioritized and allotted *before* we start our day or week. This will help us cope with the urgent needs and crises without neglecting our normal responsibilities.

3. *Keep your priorities in order.* Ask yourself: "Why am I doing this? Do I have to do it *now?* Is there something else that *must* be done first?" This will help us define personal and ministry priorities. To make sure our goals and priorities are effective, evaluate and modify them regularly.

4. *Delegate.* Ask yourself: "Is there someone who can do this job as well or better than I?" Then delegate the job to that person. Perhaps we could train someone to do an aspect of our job. Although this may take longer at the outset, it's the best way to build genuine teamwork in our groups. One big obstacle to delegation is our fear that people will let us down or make us look bad. As soon as we overcome that fear, we are free to delegate. This will give us time for other, more important things, and it will help others feel more a part of the ministry.

5. *Plan for interruptions.* People never have crises according to our schedule. Allow room in the schedule for spontaneous visits, telephone interruptions, and emergencies. A tightly packed schedule may help us feel more prepared, but it may hinder us from caring for people.

6. *Respond rather than react to crises.* One day a panicked mother called me: "I must see you right away!" (It was my day off.) Rather than react immediately with "OK, I'll be right there," I first asked some questions about the reason for her panic. I discovered that her sixteen-year-old son didn't want to take piano lessons anymore. He was being rebellious for the first time, and his

mother was petrified. I convinced her to delay our appointment until the following day.

Some situations in youth ministry will demand our immediate response. Many "crisis" situations, however, can be easily handled with thoughtful, patient investigation. We still need to respond to these needs, but we can do so by managing the crisis rather than reacting to it.

7. *Don't procrastinate.* We all have aspects of our jobs—calling that parent, visiting that hyperactive junior higher, planning that hayride—that are easy to put off. One management consultant teaches that the best way to handle these difficult matters is to do them *first.* Getting our unpleasant tasks done first avoids procrastination and enables us to move on to the more enjoyable things.

8. *Get some help.* Read books about management. Consult with people who can help you, especially those whose administrative abilities you admire. If your first thought is, "That sounds great, but I don't really have time," then you are in trouble. You need to get some managerial help.

9. *Plan for growth.* Study days, planning times, and quality time with the Lord and other people don't happen by accident. Time must be budgeted for personal reflection and study, for family and friends. Like plants, people grow only through care and a productive environment.

Take time off! The youth worker who moans (or sometimes boasts) about "thirty days without a day off" has lost perspective. God worked for six days and then rested on the seventh. Is your work more critical than his? The sabbath rest is essential if we want to maintain our health—spiritual, emotional, physical, and relational. And this rest must be on a day other than Sunday; it must be a day when our responsibilities and concerns can be left behind.

10. *Pray.* "Commit to the LORD, whatever you do, and your plans will succeed" (Prov. 16:3). Do you genuinely believe that God is in control of your life and ministry? The reality of his presence must pervade our lives as we plan and manage. We will miss one of our greatest resources if we try to plan without his purposes and presence in mind.

Management is more than a task. It's a lifelong challenge, a skill to be developed and refined. By developing management skills, we grow in effectiveness in the ministry to which we have been called. Though it costs time and effort, the results—progressive, long-term fruit, both in us and in our ministries—are more than worth it.

ENVIRONMENTAL MANAGEMENT
(UNCLUTTERING YOUR DESK)

Someone has said, "Cluttered desk—cluttered mind." When Ralph Cordiner was asked about the clean desk for which he was famous, the inquirer received a swift response: "Why shouldn't it be? Isn't one important thing enough to be doing at a time? It makes it easier to finish one task without being interrupted by another."

Taking the following steps is one helpful method of uncluttering a desk and keeping it so:

1. Clear your desk of everything related in any way to projects other than the one at hand. That one ought to be your top priority for the moment.

2. Don't permit any other items to be put on your desk until you are ready for them. This means that all projects must have a place in a file or drawer and ought to be in that place.

3. Resist temptations to leave the project you are working on for other, more appealing tasks, because of attractive interruptions or because you are tired of it. Be sure you have taken all possible action indicated before disposing of it.

4. Send it on its way, recheck your priorities, then start on the next most important project.[1]

---

[1]R. Alec MacKenzie, *The Time Trap: Managing Your Way Out,* (New York, NY: AMACOM, 1972), 67.

TIPS FOR CONQUERING "TIME WASTERS"

These common time wasters can help you to analyze your own time-management problems. The causes and solutions are merely suggestions that may help you pinpoint your own personal causes and solutions.

Time Waster	Possible Causes	Solutions
Lack of planning	Failure to see the benefit	Recognize that planning takes time but saves time in the end.
	Action orientation	Emphasize results, not activity.
	Success without it	Recognize that success is often in spite of, not because of, methods.
Lack of priorities	Lack of goals and objectives	Write down goals and objectives. Discuss priorities with subordinates.
Overcommitment	Broad interests. Confusion in priorities. Failure to set priorities.	Say no. Put first things first. Develop a personal philosophy of time. Relate priorities to a schedule of events.
Management by crisis	Lack of planning	Apply the same solution as for lack of planning
	Unrealistic time estimates	Allow more time. Allow for interruptions.
	Problem orientation	Be opportunity oriented.

Time Waster	Possible Causes	Solutions
	Reluctance of subordinates to break bad news	Encourage fast transmission of information as essential for timely corrective action.
Haste	Impatience with detail	Take time to get it right. Save the time of doing it over.
	Responding to the urgent	Distinguish between the urgent and the important.
	Lack of planning ahead	Take time to plan; it repays itself many times over.
	Attempting too much in too little time	Attempt less. Delegate more.
Paperwork and reading	Knowledge explosion	Read selectively. Learn speed reading.
	Computeritis	Manage computer data by exception.
	Failure to screen	Remember the Pareto principle. Delegate reading to subordinates.
Routine and trivia	Lack of priorities	Set and concentrate on goals. Delegate non-essentials.
	Oversurveillance of subordinates	Delegate; then give subordinates their freedom. Look to results, not details or methods.

Time Waster	Possible Causes	Solutions
	Refusal to delegate; feeling of greater security dealing with operating detail	Recognize that without delegation it is impossible to get anything done through others.
Visitors	Enjoyment of socializing	Do it elsewhere. Meet visitors outside. Suggest lunch if necessary. Hold stand-up conferences.
	Inability to say no	Screen. Say no. Be unavailable. Modify the open-door policy.
Telephone	Lack of self-discipline. Desire to be informed and involved	Screen and group calls. Be brief. Stay uninvolved with all but essentials. Manage by exception.
Meetings	Fear of responsibility for decisions. Indecision.	Make decisions without meetings. Make decisions even when some facts are missing.
	Overcommunication	Discourage unnecessary meetings. Convene only those needed.
	Poor leadership	Use agendas. Stick to the subject. Prepare concise minutes as soon as possible.
Indecision	Lack of confidence in the facts	Improve fact-finding and validating procedures.

Time Waster	Possible Causes	Solutions
	Insistence on all facts—paralysis of analysis	Accept risks as inevitable. Decide without all facts.
	Fear of the consequences of a mistake	Delegate the right to be wrong. Use mistakes as a learning process.
	Lack of a rational decision-making process	Get facts, set goals, investigate alternatives and negative consequences, make the decision, and implement it.
Lack of delegation	Fear of subordinates' inadequacy	Train. Allow mistakes. Replace if necessary.
	Fear of subordinates' competence	Delegate fully. Give credit. Insure corporate growth to maintain challenge.
	Work overload on subordinates	Balance the workload. Staff up. Reorder priorities.[2]

---

[2] Ibid., 173-176.

4.
PERSONAL PRIORITIES FOR YOUTH MINISTRY

I'm a compulsive list maker. If I want to get something done, I make a list of the steps needed to accomplish my task. On Monday mornings I make my list for the week. Sometimes I even write, "Make a list" on the top of my Monday-morning list just so that I will have something to cross out after the list is made. By crossing out item one, I feel that I have already accomplished something.

The problem with being a list maker is that I can convince myself that being organized is an end in itself. I once asked my friend's five-year-old son what he was going to do that day. Jimmy had his list: "First, I am going to build some walls [with his blocks]. Then I will knock down some walls, and then I will play with my trucks." The kid was organized; he had his list. But for what purpose?

I had to ask myself the same question. Was I organizing myself to accomplish a higher purpose, or was I simply making lists to feel organized? Was I simply building some walls and knocking them down?

Meticulous organization isn't an end in itself. But good organization can help people to grow. Finely tuned programs can be used to lead students to a deeper knowledge of Christ. High-quality administration can help create a growth environment.

We all find ourselves faced with varying degrees of organizational responsibilities. Leroy Eims summarizes these responsibilities this way: "I am responsible for two categories of work: the kind I *like* to do and the kind I *have* to do. My tendency is to do what I like and leave until later what I have to do. The problem with that scheme is that undone, unpleasant work is always pulling on my sleeve reminding me it's there."[1]

To resolve the problems of doing the things we don't want to do and the problem of seeing organization as an end in itself, we need to point to higher goals—*priorities*—the purposes behind the work we are undertaking.

PRIORITIES FOR EFFECTIVE LEADERSHIP

Effectiveness in the organization of our ministries must come first from personal choices that we have made. As was stated earlier, our youth ministries will ultimately reveal who we are. If we are list makers who organize for the sake of checking things off of our lists, then we may plan great programs even if no one comes. If we are procrastinators who avoid the jobs that *have* to be done in favor of the jobs we *like*, then we may have a lot of fun in the youth ministry, but few higher goals (like spiritual growth or family ministry) will be accomplished.

To be effective as planners, leaders, or programmers, consider three basic priorities that youth leaders should choose.

1. *Excellence.* It is said that there are three types of people: those who make things happen, those who watch while others make things happen, and those who don't know what's happening. Any youth leader who aspires to be a leader who makes things happen must commit himself or herself to excellence.

Excellence, however, doesn't start with the monthly mailer or the Sunday school lesson. Excellence starts in our personal lives. We begin with ourselves. E. D. Osborn has said, "If your aim is control, it must be self-control first. If your aim is management, it must be self-management first."[2] Leroy Eims states it even more forcefully: "The inner life of the leader will either make him or break him."[3]

We must be leaders who are committed to personal, spiritual

---

[1] Leroy Eims, *Be The Leader You Were Meant To Be*, (Wheaton, IL: Victor Books, 1975), 82.

[2] R. Alec MacKenzie, *Time Trap: Managing Your Way Out*, (New York, NY: AMACOM, 1972), 61.

[3] Eims, *Be The Leader*, 39.

disciplines. Daily time with God, a commitment to prayer, study of the Scriptures, and a sincere desire to grow as Christians should characterize our lives.

A speaker at a conference said to youth workers, "I am concerned about your commitments to excellence because so many of you are overweight." Everyone looked around with a Last-Supper "Is-it-I?" expression, but we knew what he was getting at. Our visible lack of discipline in our physical fitness would surely manifest itself in other ways in our youth ministry leadership.

Our commitment to excellence goes beyond our personal lives to our examples as leaders. We need to seek to follow Christ and exhibit our obedience so that we can join the apostle Paul in saying, "Follow me as I follow Christ."

In youth ministry, excellence in leadership means being willing to prepare ourselves for ministry, to do our homework. We must say to our co-workers, "I will work harder than any of you; I want you to push yourself even as I seek to push myself."

Excellence in youth ministry leadership means a commitment to the truth. In practical terms, this commitment means that we are more committed to lead than we are to our popularity—even with our youth group members. We summarize this commitment in our youth ministry by telling leaders, "It is more important to lead than it is to be liked." We say this because the best decision is sometimes not the popular decision. Disciplining students who misbehave, punishing those who break the rules, and choosing spiritual growth over a party atmosphere is never easy, but it's necessary for the long-term growth of our groups.

Excellence in youth ministry also means a basic commitment to maintain healthy relationships. Students, co-workers, fellow staff members, church leaders, and parents of youth all will be looking to the youth leader in one way or another. Excellence in leadership will mean a sincere commitment to keep these relationships unhindered by sin, consistent with the standards of Scripture, and full of love, forgiveness, mercy, and grace.

Excellence is high-demand commitment. It is also a lifetime commitment, but it is a goal to shoot for in our personal lives, our leadership, and our relationships to others. It is an underlying personal priority that can affect the people and programs of our ministries.

> If a task is once begun
> Never leave it till it's done;
> Be the labor great or small
> Do it well or not at all.

That's excellence—committing ourselves to do the best we can possibly do. It's an attitude that will help us and our ministries to flourish.

2. *Vision.* Where are we going? Where is our ministry going? Effective youth ministry leadership requires us to be people with vision so that programs, retreats, or activities are pointing toward a goal. So what is our vision?

Before establishing a vision or direction for the youth ministry, we must again look at ourselves: what is our vision for our own lives? Where do we see ourselves going? Do we feel locked in to youth ministry?

In his book, *Lectures To My Students,* the great Baptist preacher Charles Haddon Spurgeon exhorts seminarians to avoid the ministry unless they had the feeling "I can do nothing else." By this, he was referring to a God-given sense of calling that nothing else (no secular job) would satisfy. Unfortunately, some men and women have misconstrued Spurgeon's urging; they stay in the ministry because they can do "nothing else." They feel locked in, unable to get a job in the secular world, so they persevere in spite of frustration and in spite of a chronic lack of vision. If we are in this position, we owe it to ourselves and to our ministries to reevaluate. If we have no vision for our lives or ministries, both will suffer.

Tony Campolo speaks to the problems of errant vision for youth leaders in his article "Hidden Reasons Behind the Revolving Door Syndrome": "Many youth workers enter the ministry to satisfy emotional needs that characterize immaturity. As they outgrow these immature emotional needs which they have gratified in youth ministry, they find that youth work loses the capacity to excite them".[4] As their vision for themselves changes and matures,

---

[4]Tony Campolo, "Hidden Reasons Behind the Revolving Door Syndrome," *Youthworker Journal* (Summer 1984), 24.

they may find that they entered youth ministry under the wrong pretenses. When their personal vision is better established, they know how to proceed.

All of us need to be willing to work through our sense of personal vision as it relates to youth ministry. Our sense of calling to youth ministry can't be a disconnected appendage to the rest of our lives. We must be integrated people.

Our personal visions then should be combined with our ministry vision. Our commitment to our vision for ministry is often the thing that will keep us going. Long-term youth worker Les Christie addresses one of the perpetual problems youth leaders face: "Usually a youth worker starts out with great intentions. But sooner or later he gets so bogged down in meetings and programs that he no longer has time for the young people who are the object of his youth ministry."[5]

What keeps us from getting bogged down? Our sense of ministry vision. Others might use words like goals or objectives or purpose statements, but the meaning is the same: we need to know the target; we must try to establish an end result toward which we are aiming.

Some people establish their goals or vision on numbers: "We would like a youth ministry with 150 students." Others use more spiritual terminology: "Our purpose is to instruct students how to walk by faith." A proper answer probably lies somewhere in between. Quality (measured by things like witnessing at school, involvement in discipleship groups, or service to the needy) is balanced by a vision for quantity (having twenty-five percent of our Sunday school attenders witnessing on a regular basis at school).

Disciplining oneself to establish a ministry vision is a crucial priority because it offers direction. A ministry without goals . . .

   . . . covers too much ground

   . . . majors in the minors

   . . . has a tendency to ramble

   . . . may not be related to life needs

[5] Les Christie, *Getting a Grip on Time Management*, (Wheaton, IL: Victor Books, 1984), 7.

. . . has few or no results[6]

David Jacquith has observed it another way: "Good results without good planning come from good luck, not good management."[7]

We need to see where we are going—both personally and in our youth ministries. We must commit ourselves to developing our sense of vision. It must be a priority.

3. *Endurance.* Although teenagers love to be associated with leaders who are dynamic or funny or charismatic, I believe that students' greater need is for leaders who will stick with them over their adolescent years. Effective leadership and organization in the youth ministry calls us to make endurance a personal priority.

We've already discussed some of the external things we can do to foster our own longevity in youth ministry, but the personal commitment to endurance must come from within. To "finish the course" (2 Tim. 4:7) with youth ministry (and by this I mean a minimum of a three-year commitment) requires an active choice on our part.

We must learn to endure in spite of apparent failures and setbacks. Throughout my years as a youth worker, I have drawn great strength from the example of Abraham Lincoln:

> He grew up on an isolated farm and had only one year of formal education. In those early years he was exposed to barely half a dozen books. In 1832 he lost his job and was defeated in the race for the Illinois legislature. In 1833 he failed in business. In 1834 he was elected to the state legislature, but in 1835 his sweetheart died, and in 1836 he had a nervous breakdown. In 1838 he was defeated for nomination for Congress. In 1846 he was elected to Congress but in 1848 lost the re-nomination. In 1849 he was rejected for a federal land officer appointment, and in 1854 he was defeated for the Senate. In 1856 he was defeated for the nomination for vice-president, and in 1858 he was again defeated for the Senate.[8]

Abe Lincoln was one of our greatest presidents because he endured. He didn't let defeat or failure keep him down.

Many of us in youth ministry know defeat and feelings of

---

[6] Ibid., 20.

[7] MacKenzie, Time Trap, 39.

[8] Ted Engstrom, *Pursuit of Excellence,* (Grand Rapids, MI: Zondervan, 1984), 76-77.

failure. Like parents of teenagers, we can sometimes look at the students we are supposed to be influencing and say, "Where am I going wrong?" But we can endure because "He who promised is faithful" (Heb. 10:23). God will bring about his good purposes in our lives and in the lives of the young people we are working with—even through discouraging setbacks.

Making endurance a personal priority has special meaning for me because it is this basic commitment that enabled me to stick it out in youth ministry. I didn't have the stereotypical youth ministry gifts—music, athletics, joke telling, speaking. I followed a youth minister who did, so naturally I was nervous about the comparisons against which I would look weak.

Nevertheless, I committed myself to the youth ministry. At the outset, I committed myself to seeing one generation through high school. There were plenty of failures, some hurtful moments, some times of doubting, but endurance has paid off. In the past ten years, I have seen students grow to be pastors, missionaries, effective husbands and wives, and solid Christians who are leading others to Christ and discipling them. Perhaps I would have seen it happen in a shorter period of time, but for me, the joy of hearing "that my children are walking in the truth" (3 John 4) has made every hour of endurance worth it.

THE BENEFITS OF LONGEVITY

Sticking with youth ministry for a long time has many positive results:

- Effectiveness with young people will increase because the students trust you. Students who have come to our youth group from other churches with unstable youth ministries have said, "It's just good to know you'll be here."

- Results (a hard-to-find commodity in youth work) will become more apparent as those who have graduated return to join the youth team. When students come back after two or three years of college and tell how essential the youth group was in their growth, it has motivated me to keep working with teenagers.

- Parents will grow in their trust, which builds more continuity between family and youth ministry.

- Lay leaders will be trained over a period to time with one consistent philosophy and strategy of ministry. This allows for greater unity and long-term growth.
- The youth minister will be a professional who is, in effect, the church's expert on adolescents.

As we commit ourselves to personal and ministry excellence, our organizational responsibilities will take on new meaning as we try to grow. As we commit ourselves to the development of a personal and ministry vision, our administrative responsibilities will become important because we can see where we are going and where we would like to go.

Our final commitment—the priority of endurance—will help us see our programming and management as a progressive task. We can look to the long-term results of weeks or years of ministry rather than to the "miracle-meeting" syndrome that expects everything to happen in one meeting or through one program.

5.
CHALLENGES OF CHURCH YOUTH MINISTRY

After seven years on the staff of Youth for Christ, my friend Roy entered seminary. He wanted a better theological foundation for ministry and a youth ministry position in a local church.

While attending seminary, Roy took several youth ministry courses and attended two conferences on youth ministry in an effort to stay fresh. When he graduated, he became an associate minister at a church within his denomination. He was responsible for the youth groups, with additional part-time preaching, counseling, and visitation duties.

When Roy began working with the youth groups, he felt prepared. His philosophical and theological "guns" were loaded. He had lots of ideas for programs. He was ready to go. That was September.

By late November, Roy was *very* discouraged. A few months of flat programming, disinterested kids, and hassles from parents had tired him out. On November 22, he wrote in his diary: "Working with church youth is more difficult than I ever expected."

Youth ministry in the local church differs from the ministries of the para-church organizations. It differs from the idealistic models often presented in manuals and seminars.

HOW IS CHURCH YOUTH MINISTRY DIFFERENT?

The first step toward solving the problems inherent in local church youth ministry is identifying the tensions that youth ministers and leaders will face. In what way is *church* ministry to young people unique?

The responsibilities are different. When Roy accepted the position of associate minister, he took on a host of responsibilities unrelated to youth ministry. Preparation for a monthly sermon, six to eight hours per week of counseling, and two or three trips to the hospital each week were reminders that young people were not his only focus. These other duties competed for his time and attention.

While all leaders work within systems of relationships, authority, and communication, tensions arise for the youth minister because his or her "systems" are often broader and larger. My friend John, a Young Life staff member, has one superior to whom he reports. He has one boss. The church youth worker, on the other hand, has one superior on the organizational chart but also has parents, elders (or deacons), and sometimes even the young people themselves who function as "superiors."

The complexity of relationships and the anxiety of multiple responsibilities are facts which are in direct conflict with much that is taught or written about youth ministry. Many youth ministry ideals assume that the leader has forty or more hours per week to dedicate to youth work; this is seldom the case in church ministry.

The kids are different. Remember Roy? One of the factors that discouraged him most in his ministry was disinterested kids. Church youth, while representing one of the great resources of the church, are also one of the greatest challenges to the church.

First, it may mean that the kids are "Christianized." Many of the kids in church youth groups come from Christian families, have always attended Sunday school, and some may even attend a Christian school. These students know the Bible stories, can repeat doctrines verbatim, and can give pat answers to even the most thought-provoking questions. As a result, youth workers face the challenge of working with young people who say, "I dare you to teach me anything new."

Second, some teenagers from Christian families may be attending the youth group against their will. They come into a youth group meeting, sit in the back row, and fold their arms. They may write notes, talk to their friends, or sleep. When asked if they want to be in the youth group, they reply, "No, but our parents told us that if we want to be able to go out other nights, we have to go to youth group." Any way you look at it, these students are entering the group through circumstances that will not make life easy for their youth leaders. Progress will be difficult.

Third, the interrelationship between the church and the youth group means that the youth leader will be the target of many parental hopes or demands. "We are really looking forward to the changes *you* can make in our children." One youth minister was asked why he was spending time with a rebellious youth who had abandoned his parents' faith two years earlier. He said that the church elders had told him that the youth's parents had served in the church so faithfully that the church was obligated to try to reach this boy. Such pressures on this youth minister made his job very difficult.

Problems with teenagers in the youth group may be compounded if the youth minister is just another in a succession of youth ministers. The high turnover of youth workers in the local church often means that the responsiveness in many young people has been destroyed through broken relationships and unfulfilled promises.

The task is different. Jack, a veteran youth worker with a local para-church ministry, spends up to four days per week meeting with unchurched students, sharing the gospel message. Church youth workers usually can't do this without being accused of abandoning the young people of the church. The primary task of the para-church organization is evangelism; the task of the church youth worker is nurturing.

For the church youth worker, the challenge is to work with those who know the gospel *intellectually*, but who need to *personalize* the faith of their parents. Taking teenagers through this painstaking and gradual process demands commitment and patience. This commitment to nurture youth is made even more complex because the church youth leader must be versatile in reaching teenagers who are on a variety of spiritual levels. Many youth groups will include the *disillusioned* (who want nothing to do with Christianity), the *searchers* (who want to know God but don't know how), the *fence-sitters* (who, like chameleons, modify their behavior to fit their environment), the *neutrals* (whose apathy about everything makes if difficult to know what they believe), and the *disciples* (whose zeal to follow Jesus often alienates them from their peers).

The leader's versatility is further tested as students fluctuate across the spiritual spectrum on a weekly or monthly basis. The task of the church youth minister then becomes the patient tracking of these young people until they come to a firm commitment to Jesus Christ and to the pursuit of a Christian lifestyle.

POSITIVE STEPS FOR CHURCH YOUTH MINISTRY

Recognizing the unique aspects of church youth work is only the first step toward effective discipleship, growth, and outreach. Three other actions must follow.

Define our target: church youth. Tim has an incredible youth ministry. He leads a discipleship Bible study with church youth and an evangelistic group at the local high school; he coordinates separate programs for the churched and unchurched because he recognizes the different needs of the two groups. Tim is an exceptional man; he is also very tired.

Most of us have to decide whether to work with the church youth or with the unchurched. We don't have the abilities, gifts, or time to do both. Yet we in the church youth ministry are sometimes afraid of stating, "I am called by God to work with *church* youth." Perhaps we are afraid of the implications, or we may fear someone will accuse us of having lost our burden for the unsaved. Nevertheless, effective youth ministry in the church requires that the church youth become the priority and the focus. This concentration, however, carries with it certain weighty implications.

This mind-set implies a willingness to accept and work within the church "system" mentioned earlier. We all would love to visit high school campuses every day, but our job requires us to maintain the youth budget, plan the hayride, book the speaker for the retreat, go to the staff meeting, attend the evening service, meet with the elders, or write a staff report. The system in which God has placed us means that we must take all of our responsibilities into account as we set our personal and ministry goals.

Making the church youth a priority also implies a commitment to work with parents and families. Like Tim Jack, high school pastor at Grace Community Church in Sun Valley, California, we must see our ministries in the context of families. As he stated in an interview, "We are seeking to help families in their ministry to youth, not to replace it with ours" (*Youthletter*, April 1983, p. 31).

This commitment can be frightening at times. For example, one father was angry with me because his sixteen-year-old son was not witnessing for Christ at his high school. I knew that I could either be silent and take the blows, or I could overcome my fears and speak the truth. I spoke up: "Sir, do you witness to your friends, at work?" He mumbled something about everyone already knowing he was a Christian. I reminded him that unless he was willing to set an example, it would be very difficult for me to get his son to do evangelism. Effective ministry to the students requires courageous ministry with the parents.

Our commitment to church youth requires patience with them as they grow. Christian teenagers are curious, and the sheltered environment they are raised in often increases this curiosity about what "the world" is really like. As a result, they might experiment and test the waters of the secular world while they profess to follow Christ. This spiritual inconsistency should be challenged, but the ability to be merciful and understanding of these students' curiosity is also important.

Finally, a stated commitment to church youth implies the support of the other leaders in the church. Bernie, a church youth minister, has an effective ministry to church youth, but he lives under the constant pressure of comparison with the local area's Campus Life outreach. Were it not for the complete support and encouragement of the church's other pastors and the lay leadership, Bernie probably would move on to another church.

Effective ministry to church teenagers requires that others in the church recognize that the youth group is a demanding job and requires the youth leader's primary attention. If the church expects the youth worker to give 100 percent of his or her time to church growth and 100 percent of his or her time to outreach, the youth worker will face an impossible and unreachable goal.

Define our role: pastor to youth. John Musselman, former Minister of Youth at the Coral Ridge Presbyterian Church in Fort Lauderdale, Florida, asks this question: "Are we the *pastor* to our youth?" If we are, he insists, then we should be equipping *them* to do their own God-given ministries.

This helpful piece of biblical advice (according to Ephesians 4:11–13) can transform our perspective of ourselves and our ministries. Instead of trying to be everything in our youth ministry, we are responsible to be the pastor to youth, the equipper. Our responsibility is to teach them, to exemplify a Christian lifestyle, and to pray for them so that they—as members of the body of Christ, which the Christian students are—can do their ministry. Rather than being docile observers who are entertained and cajoled, our students can become the active participants who "own" the ministry.

Each September, I share my vision with our high school students. As I share my dreams for evangelism at their high school campuses, I explain my role as equipper: "It isn't my job to reach these students. It *is* my job to make sure that *you* are equipped to do this outreach. Reaching these students is your responsibility. If you aren't equipped, then I am failing. But if you are equipped and you don't act, then the failure is yours."

This changed definition of my role has brought great joy and fulfillment as I have had the opportunity to see students rise to the challenge. To see Andy teach Sunday school or to see Brett start his own evangelistic Bible study gives me much greater joy than doing it myself. The joy that John expressed in seeing his "children walking in the truth" is available to those of us who equip our youth to do their own ministries.

Define our goal: to challenge for growth. We in church youth work are always in danger of compromising the goals of teaching and admonishing (Col. 1:28). However, if we are to stimulate our youth to grow toward completeness in Christ, we must resist the temptation to compromise.

Some of us fall prey to the compromise of entertainment. We convince ourselves that a bigger and better program (with large crowds, of course) means that we are succeeding with our young people. A problem emerges, however, when it becomes apparent that the quality of the entertainment—rather than commitment to Christ—has become the criteria for attendance and participation.

Perry had an active program that reached 250 or more teenagers (an amazing fact in the Northeast), but he cut his program way back. Why? "I realized that pulling off the program was becoming the goal," he said, "and I saw my fellow leaders expending all of their energies there rather than in ministry to the kids."

Others of us fall prey to compromising our goals because we become preoccupied with popularity. I am over thirty years old, fifteen years out of high school, and happily married—yet it really bothers me when a teenager in my youth group doesn't like me. I try to argue with myself: "Why does this bother me? I don't need the approval of a fifteen year old!" But it still bothers me. I like to be liked.

The compromise occurs when we let this desire to be liked by the kids (and their parents) overcome our biblical priorities of growth, accountability, and challenge. We simply can't be everyone's buddy. Effective ministry to youth in the church context requires that we define our priorities clearly. Christian growth is more important than being entertained. Being the leader is more important than being liked. When these priorities are defined, we are free to challenge students and parents to grow toward maturity in Christ.

Students need to know that following Christ isn't fun and games, or a search for self-fulfillment. Following Christ demands commitment; following Christ is costly. Charles Atlas coined the phrase, "No pain; no gain." Young people believe this. They are willing to practice through the grueling summer heat in order to play football. They will spend all of their money and much of their time to pursue their desire to play guitars or synthesizers. They believe that a worthwhile goal is worth the cost.

If church youth aren't met with the challenge to follow Christ, they will seek challenges elsewhere. We in the church must not be afraid to present the commitment and cost of following Christ. Our groups may decrease in size, but the depth of growth in the students will surpass our expectations.

In 1978, we started teen mission teams (see chapter 17) at our church. We didn't know how our young people would accept the concept of paying for the opportunity to work, so we proceeded slowly. They only had to write a brief testimony and raise half of the trip's cost. Over the years these teams have grown, largely because we have added more and more challenge each year. Now students have to raise all their support; they have to write an application and four other reports; they have to participate in a training weekend; they have to memorize Scripture, recruit prayer supporters, and speak in services. Some summers, over eighty percent of our high school students have applied for teams. The basic rule has proven itself: The more we challenge them, the more they respond and grow as a result.

Youth ministry in the local church *is* different. We no doubt have much to learn from the expertise of the para-church youth professionals and the nationwide seminars. Local church youth ministry, however, must go a few steps further. The unique aspects of our churches, our youth, and our ministries must be identified, implemented, and integrated into our specific setting to make our divine calling come alive in the challenging but uniquely satisfying environment of the local church.

Resources for Part I

PERSONAL GROWTH

Bolles, Richard Nelson. *The Three Boxes of Life*. Berkeley, California: Ten Speed Press, 1978.

_____. *What Color Is Your Parachute?* Berkeley, California: Ten Speed Press, 1976.

Campbell, David. *If You Don't Know Where You're Going, You'll Probably End Up Somewhere Else*. Niles, Illinois: Argus Publications, 1974.

_____. *If I'm in Charge Here, Why Is Everybody Laughing?* Niles, Illinois: Argus Publications, 1980.

Campolo, Anthony. *The Success Fantasy*. Wheaton, Illinois: Victor Books, 1980.

Carlson, Dwight L. *Run and Not Be Weary*. Old Tappan, New Jersey: Fleming H. Revell, 1974.

Dayton, Edward R., and Engstrom, Ted W. *Strategy For Living*. Glendale, California: G/L Regal Books, 1976.

Engstrom, Ted W. *The Pursuit of Excellence*. Grand Rapids: Zondervan Publishing House, 1984.

Foster, Richard J. *The Celebration of Discipline*. San Francisco: Harper & Row, 1978.

_____. *The Freedom of Simplicity*. San Francisco: Harper & Row, 1981.

Larson, Bruce. *The One and Only You*. Waco, Texas: Word Books, 1976.

MacDonald, Gordon. *Ordering Your Private World*. Nashville, Tennessee: Thomas Nelson, 1985.

Miller, Arthur F., and Mattson, Ralph T. *The Truth About You*. Old Tappan, New Jersey: Fleming H. Revell, 1977.

Navone, John. *A Theology of Failure*. New York: Paulist Press, 1974.

Nouwen, Henri. *The Genesee Diary*. Garden City, New York: Doubleday and Company, Inc., 1976.

Peters, Tom, and Austin, Nancy. *A Passion for Excellence*. New York: Random House, 1985.

Schaller, Lyle E. *Survival Tactics in the Parish*. Nashville, Tennessee: Abingdon Press, 1977.

Sider, Ronald (ed.). *Living More Simply*. Downers Grove, Illinois: InterVarsity Press, 1980.

Snyder, Howard. *The Problem of Wineskins*. Downers Grove, Illinois: InterVarsity Press, 1975.

White, John. *The Golden Cow*. Downers Grove, Illinois: InterVarsity Press, 1979.

MANAGEMENT AND YOUTH MINISTRY
MANAGEMENT

Banks, Robert. *The Tyranny of Time*. Downers Grove, Illinois: InterVarsity Press, 1983.

Christie, Les. *Getting a Grip on Time Management*. Wheaton, Illinois: Victor Books, 1984.

Drucker, Peter. *Management*. New York: Harper & Row, 1973.

Hughes, Charles L. *Goal-Setting*. New York: American Management Association, 1965.

Hummel, Charles E. *Tyranny of the Urgent*. Downers Grove, Illinois: InterVarsity Press, 1967.

Morgan, John S., and Philip, J.R. *You Can't Manage Alone*. Grand Rapids: Zondervan Publishing House, 1985.

Reinhardt, James. *Time Management for the Youth Minister*. Washington, D.C.: National CYO Federation, 1980.

Rice, Wayne (ed.). *110 Tips, Time-Savers, and Tricks of the Trade*. El Cajon, California: Youth Specialties, 1984.

Sparks, Lee (ed.). *The Youth Worker's Personal Management Handbook*. Loveland, Colorado: Group Books, 1985.

PERSONAL AND FAMILY LIFE

Bailey, Robert W. *Coping With Stress in the Minister's Home*. Nashville, Tennessee: Broadman Press, 1979.

MacDonald, Gail. *High Call, High Privilege*. Wheaton, Illinois: Tyndale House Publishers, Inc., 1981.

MacDonald, Gordon. *The Effective Father*. Wheaton, Illinois: Tyndale House Publishers, Inc., 1977.

_____. *Magnificent Marriage*. Wheaton, Illinois: Tyndale House Publishers, Inc., 1976.

Minirth, Frank. *The Workaholic and His Family*. Grand Rapids: Baker Book House, 1981.

Nordland, Frances. *The Unprivate Life of the Pastor's Wife.* Chicago: Moody Press, 1972.

Oswald, Roy M. *Married to the Minister.* Washington, D.C.: The Alban Institute, 1980.

Senter, Ruth. *So You're the Pastor's Wife.* Grand Rapids: Zondervan Publishing House, 1979.

Taylor, Alice. *How To Be a Minister's Wife and Love It.* Grand Rapids: Zondervan Publishing House, 1968.

Part II

ORGANIZING YOUTH MINISTRY— PHILOSOPHICAL FOUNDATIONS

I suppose I was about two years into my youth ministry experience before I started thinking anything about issues like "philosophies of youth ministry." For me such thinking came just at the right time. After two years of programs, activities, meetings, and retreats, I was feeling pretty tired. When an older peer asked me why I was in youth work, I was forced to probe for answers. What exactly was I trying to accomplish? How would I accomplish it?

Jay Kesler, former president of Youth for Christ/USA and now president of Taylor University, refers to this "why" as the "theology of youth ministry":

> Your personal theology will have an effect on everything you do in youth work. It will influence the type of message you bring, the response you expect, the progress of the youth with whom you minister, your method of counseling, your attitude toward others, and

how you measure results. In short, all we do relates to what we actually believe.[1]

What do we actually believe about youth ministry? Are we just youth advisors? Is our role to provide programs to keep students out of trouble until they reach mature adulthood? Why are we doing what we are doing?

Our philosophy of youth ministry (or, in Kesler's terminology, our theology of youth ministry) will have a significant part in helping us organize and plan. Our meetings, activities, and events in the youth ministry will be a reflection of what we believe our ministry can accomplish.

In the broadest terms, youth ministry exists for four philosophical reasons:

1. To minister to the needs of adolescents, students who are at a special growth phase of their lives.

2. To address the gospel in terms understandable to students in this growth phase, seeking to incorporate them into the body of Christ.

3. To minister as a support and complement to families of these students.

4. To build the body of Christ through the training and nurturing of believers and the evangelization of non-believers.

To some degree, Chapter 5 began addressing some of the philosophical issues, but Part II addresses these underlying philosophies in a more direct way. Chapters 6, 7, and 9 deal with the needs and the spiritual growth of students. Chapter 10 addresses the need for family ministry, and chapters 8 and 9 deal with some specific ways that we must seek to build the body of Christ, both through students and through lay leaders.

Although Part II may address some issues related to direct programming, it will do that in the context of analyzing what we believe youth ministry can and should be doing. This analysis, then, becomes the foundation on which to plan programs.

---

[1] "Determining Your Theology of Youth Ministry," in *The Youth Leader's Sourcebook,* Gary Dausey, ed. (Grand Rapids, MI: Zondervan, 1983), 23.

6.
NEEDS OF YOUNG PEOPLE

When we try to determine our theological/philosophical basis for youth ministry, we look, of course, to Scripture. We at first have difficulty finding answers related to youth ministry because Jesus didn't have a youth ministry. To call his band of twelve his "youth group" is unfair to the text. The first century didn't have an adolescent culture as we know it.

However, we do learn something about all the facets of Jesus' growth. During his youth years, Jesus "grew in wisdom and stature, and in favor with God and men" (Luke 2:52). The example of Jesus points us to multidimensional growth that covers it all:

1. Intellectual growth: "Jesus grew in wisdom"

2. Physical growth: "and stature"

3. Spiritual growth: "and in favor with God"

4. Social growth: "and men."

Luke 2:52 can't be taken in isolation from the rest of Scripture as a mandate for a ministry that is equally balanced in all of these four areas. The Scriptures themselves assert *priorities:* obviously spiritual growth is more important than physical growth. But growth is a total unit; the various facets of growth work together. We cultivate our intellects and we work for good relationships because they work together to help us toward spiritual growth. We don't grow exclusively in one area without also growing in another.

Jesus' growth, summarized in Luke 2:52, provides us with a

good theological example to consider as we build a basis for programming and meeting needs. Before we start planning our activities, Bible studies, or meetings, we must take into account all the growth taking place in our students and all the growth we would like to see in their lives.

BALANCING NEEDS AND PROGRAMS

As we address the various growth dimensions of our young people, we need to be asking some specific questions to help us be realistic about the programs we plan.

1. *Who are we trying to reach?* We already discussed the significant difference between trying to reach an unchurched student and winning a religious rebel. Even within the church, the needs of students vary greatly. As I look at our youth ministry, I am overwhelmed by the diversity:

- The students in our youth ministry range in age from twelve to nineteen (some youth groups have a larger span if they include collegians).

- They come from a dozen communities and twenty-one high schools and junior high schools.

- They come from diverse family backgrounds; single parents, stepparents, Christian homes, non-Christian homes.

- There are young *men* and young *women* (need I say more about diversity?).

- Some students don't separate personal faith from going to church with mom or dad; others are genuine believers; still others are rebellious or apathetic or uninformed.

- Some have been in our youth group and church all of their lives so that nothing we offer is exciting or new; others have just joined from churches that had no youth group, and they are excited about anything.

How can any program meet the diverse needs of such a broad range of students? A seminar on dating will leave some students out, and a discussion about the biblical view of abortion will meet needs for a few. But any way we look at it, the needs vary from one student to another.

One year our church was building a new sanctuary and classrooms, and the space available for our meetings was very limited. As a result, we combined our junior high and senior high ministries for "Super Week" (our four-evening equivalent of youth Vacation Bible School). We had a good program, an excellent speaker, some student testimonies, and a lot of fun, but by the middle of the week, the older students stopped coming. By the end of the week, the audience was seventh graders to ninth graders and only a few committed high school students. What had happened? We had tried to reach too large a group, and the social needs of the older students hadn't been met. As a result, they had withdrawn.

Very few programs can meet specific needs for a broad diversity of students. Programs that do are often one-way programs (speaker to audience or musician to audience) and may meet needs only superficially.

Most youth groups specialize rather than try to get all of the students together at once. Junior high ministry is separated from senior high ministry (which is separated from college age ministry). The young men are separated from the the young women (especially when we talk about sex); the Sunday school classes might include classes for each age group.

The rationale for such specialization isn't so much that the needs change so dramatically over the years (although a junior high boy and twelfth-grade girl are very different) but rather that the social needs are so great. Psychologists refer to teenagers as having "other-directed" personalities: what others think about them and how they respond to them is *the* most important part of their lives. Thus a student's preoccupation with others in the group often will keep him or her from responding at all—even if the speaker or topic is profound.

Not only do we have to specialize because of the diversity of students already in our youth group, but we also need to plan for the student who is new to our group and has never been to church. Duffy Robbins, youth ministry professor at Eastern College, voiced this dilemma: "How do you lead a Bible study when you have church kids who have memorized John 3:16 alongside of the searching non-Christian kid who thinks John 3:16 is the bathroom on the third floor?"

Again the answer calls for specialization. Evangelistic Bible studies or low-key spiritual activities may help incorporate such students into the group so that they will be willing to learn more. But unless we meet these non-Christian students where they are, they are not likely to come back.

I'm not against big group meetings; they can meet needs for intellectual, physical, spiritual, and social growth too. Too often, however, we equate big activities with meeting lots of needs.

2. *How will we try to reach these students?* The adage "you can draw more flies with honey than with vinegar" applies here. Very few students will respond to activities that are advertised as being "challenging," at least at the outset. More will respond to terms like "fun," a "blast," or "exciting." We have to design our programs to meet the needs of students.

Sometimes large-group programs can provide an exciting "crowd mentality" that will let students be proud to bring their friends. In our outreach efforts, students get excited about the program, and they may commit themselves to coming. When asked to bring friends to an event, students often respond, "Well, who else is coming?" Translation: I will come and I don't care if it's a small group, but I don't want to bring friends unless a crowd is guaranteed.

• Big programs usually don't meet the deepest needs of students. The overweight girl who wants help in losing a few pounds certainly won't share this in a large group. The student from outside the group won't express deep spiritual interest in front of a sea of unfamiliar faces.

To meet needs, youth ministry must offer small groups where caring, discipleship, and growth can take place. Effective youth ministry is most often done one-on-one, making it necessary to have a staff team to share the load.

This is the message of youth ministry veteran E. G. von Trutzschler:

The most effective way to meet kids one-on-one is to go places they go, and do things with them. Many youth pastors are just hirelings—they produce a program. A youth pastor with a shepherding mentality, rather than that of a hireling, will produce a ministry. He wants to accomplish several things. First he wants to give his young people a taste of what he has—a personal faith in Christ. Secondly, he wants to help them mature and begin grooming them for the future—training and developing them so that they, too, can minister.[1]

A balanced program of large group, small group, specialty group (men/women, etc.), and one-on-one ministry is the best way to provide the maximum number of avenues to meet intellectual, physical, spiritual, and social needs.

3. *What needs will we try to meet?* Can any one program or meeting meet all four areas of growth needs? I don't think so. Instead, we must choose which needs we are aiming at, and then we can choose the best approach to meet those needs.

Last year we began a monthly outreach meeting that featured athletics, drama, rock music, and a speaker. The goal was to attract students who didn't attend church. We met that goal, but in the process, some of our core students became disinterested because their needs for fellowship and comradery were not being met at these big meetings. The solution? We added at other times some activities that were "body building" rather than evangelistic. If we had tried to meet our students' fellowship needs at the outreach meeting, the outreach would have been compromised.

Before we organize a program, we need to look realistically at what needs we can meet through our groups, our budgets, and our personnel. A discipleship Bible study will not meet the spiritual needs of students who are not yet Christians. A bike trip together may alienate students who are non-athletic. A special Father's Day activity will not succeed if sixty-five percent of our students are from single-parent homes.

We also must target specific activities—especially those activities geared to reach new or fringe students—to meet needs for a sense of *acceptance*. Although the spiritual dimension is our highest goal, social acceptance is more important in the mind of the

---

[1] "Youth Ministry is More Than a Meeting," in *The Youth Leader's Sourcebook*, Gary Dausey, ed. (Grand Rapids, MI: Zondervan, 1983), 39–50.

student. Just as the starving person asks the missionary concerned only about saving souls, "Will there be bread in heaven?," the average teenager, preoccupied with a desire to be liked, will ask, "Will there be *friends* in heaven?"

"Adults too easily forget how disastrous it is when a young person blows his chances for group acceptance," writes Tony Campolo in *The Success Fantasy*. "Should it take place in a church gathering, there is a strong probability that the young person will never come back to the church again!"[2]

The bottom line is this: no matter how stimulating our teaching may be and no matter how appealing our program may be, the student comes to an activity with one basic question: Will I be accepted? If we don't plan with this need in mind, we may find ourselves with attractive programs that don't draw students.

4. *Are the needs I'm trying to meet ongoing or one-time needs?* Some needs are not the primary responsibility of the youth group. Intellectual growth and physical fitness are traditionally the responsibility of the school system (although if we are working with a high number of dropouts, we may consider offering a remedial reading program or a GED [graduate equivalency diploma] program as part of our youth ministry). The youth ministry has higher degrees of responsibility for social needs and spiritual growth.

Even within these categories, some needs can be addressed once or twice throughout the year without becoming a regular part of the ministry. Seminars that we have hosted about leadership, improving your study habits, and dating have addressed a variety of intellectual and social needs (from a spiritual perspective), but they have occurred once in the year.

Other needs have been a constant part of our ministry planning. The need for social acceptance is ongoing, as is the need for spiritual growth in the basics of faith. These needs are harder to measure, but they are continual needs that should be factored into the program.

Some programs will meet more needs than the program is targeted to meet. A weekly Bible study can be targeted to meet a

---

[2]Tony Campolo, *The Success Fantasy*, (Wheaton, IL: Victor Books, 1950), 51.

need for spiritual growth, but the relationships within that study can generate growth between peers (social needs) and can challenge the student to think more deeply about God (seeing faith from a viewpoint that is intellectually rational).

We always should try to meet as many needs as possible in our programs. Extended time together—twelve hours on an "all-nighter" (where we are locked in all night, without sleep), thirty-six hours in a "Planned Famine," or more than fifty hours on a retreat—gives us opportunities to encourage growth in every area.

As we try to meet the needs of our young people, we need to become aware of where they are hurting, understand what they need from us, and then try to address this through our relationships and programs. All of this means that we stay in close touch with the young people and the world out of which they come.

7.
KEEPING FRESH

Every youth leader agrees conceptually with the premise that youth programs should be designed to meet the needs of students. The question, however, then becomes, "What are these needs?" As I have grown older, I have seen a gradual rift between my needs and their needs. In the earliest experiences I had as a youth leader, I was nineteen years old. If I designed programs that met my needs, I would come fairly close to meeting the needs of at least some of my students.

Now I am over thirty. How can I keep current with student needs? How can I make sure that our programs meet their needs even though they will seldom meet mine anymore?

Over a dozen years ago, Merton Strommen released a book that has become a youth ministry classic—*Five Cries of Youth*. In it, he described the various pressures on students: loneliness, the family, peers, and other related themes. He identified these "cries" of youth and then urged church youth groups to respond.[1]

Our task is the same: to identify our students' "cries" and then to respond. We *must* do this if our youth ministries are to be at all relevant to the teens we are trying to reach. If we don't respond, young people will find their own alternatives, as the Norman/Harris report of 1981 summarized: "Since most adults don't

---

[1]Merton Strommen, *Five Cries of Youth*, (New York, NY: Harper & Row, 1974).

really understand what teens face in school, kids learn to devise their own solutions for survival."[2]

We don't want our students thinking that we don't understand their worlds. We don't want them *surviving* by devising their own solutions (which may hurt them over a long period). We want to know where they are coming from, what pressures they are facing, and then to address these issues. We want our teenagers to know that the Christian life and biblical principles are relevant and can help them in their own lives. To do this, we must work hard to keep fresh in our understanding of teenage growth characteristics, the teenager's world, and the specific world of our youth.

THE TEENAGER'S WORLDS

Keeping current with today's teenager is no easy task because they live in several separate but overlapping worlds. Their schools, their families, their peers, and even the youth group all make up different worlds that can influence their behavior and attitudes.

1. *The school.* An average teenager will spend between fifteen percent and twenty-five percent of any week at school. (It's a much higher percentage of their waking hours). Classes, extra-curricular activities, time to hang around, and sports all play a significant part in the teenager's life. It is at school where students develop their friendships, mold their values, and form their ideas about priorities and life.

Keeping fresh requires that we put ourselves where our students live. According to the town or city, the schedule of the youth leader, and the policies of individual principals, going on campus may or may not be an option for you. Some administrators allow youth leaders on campus during the day; others forbid it. If we are not allowed on campus for lunch or to sit in on classes, we can still be creative:

- Go to a PTA meeting with parents from the youth group.

- Go to school athletic events that are open to the public.

- Volunteer to assist as a coach or tutor.

[2] Jane Norman and Myron L. Harris, *The Private Life of the American Teenager,* (New York, NY: Rawson Wade Publisher, 1981), 130.

- Sign up to chaperone a dance or social event.
- Become a sponsor of an extra-curricular club.

One principal allows me on campus all the time, as long as I check in at the office. I have sat in on classes, met students at the cafeteria for lunch, and even participated in teaching classes. Another principal doesn't allow me on campus, but he'll meet with me quarterly to share his views on themes and needs in the student body. When I meet with him, I always try to take the longest route through the school to his office. This way I can read bulletin boards, overhear conversations, look at the posters or stickers on lockers, and observe the variety of ways that students dress. All of it helps me understand the students I am trying to reach. In a third school system, I'm never allowed on campus. The principal doesn't like me too much, so I have to get my information about the school from other sources. At that school, I must rely more on what Jay Kesler calls "creative hanging around" after school or at athletic events.

Going into the world of the high school or junior high student does three things. It helps us see the real world in which they live. It challenges us to address the gospel to the needs we see there, and it increases our credibility with our students. As they hear us talking about their schools or their corridors or their principals, they begin to realize, "Hey, this person knows where I live."

2. *The family.* Experts still debate whether peers or parents have the greatest impact on young people. It may be that peers are getting the edge because of working parents, single-parent homes, and the general dissolution of quality relationships at home.

A variety of factors must be taken into account when we are seeking to understand our students' homes: the number of children, the status of their parents' marriage, the position of the child in the birth order, the faith of the parents, and the working status of each parent. Finances, in-laws living at home, and the configuration of the neighborhood also can play a part, as can the frequency of moves that the family has made over the life of the teenager.

Understanding the family situation is even more difficult than getting on campus. Few youth leaders are invited to sit in on family conversations. To find out about family needs that we might be able to meet, we can look to several sources:

- The students themselves (although this usually requires a lot of trust because they won't want to voice much criticism about their families)
- Honest parents (but those who talk honestly with you about their needs are often *not* the ones needing the most help)
- Others in the church (this can be helpful, but there is always the danger of gossip)
- School counselors (some are very willing to cooperate; others are very secretive, fearing that we'll only complicate problems with our religious answers)
- Unspoken messages from the students (nightmares on the retreat, extreme silence or misbehavior in the youth group, or caustic remarks about family members all could be signals of trouble at home).

Perhaps the most basic family need relates to our roles as "parent figures," especially to those students who don't have both parents living at home. Because children of a divorce or separation often end up living with their mother, male youth leaders can fill a critical role as a father figure. This ministry is people intensive—usually one-on-one—so it may be beyond the reach of some youth ministries, but it is a family need that churches must start addressing much more seriously if our young people are to grow up healthy in the family of God.

3. *Peers.* The strongest desire in many teenagers is the desire to be loved and accepted. As the teenager grows, however, even the solid family doesn't provide enough of this love. An average teenager will go outside of the home to test his or her skills at forming relationships and finding love from others. This is why the world of their peers is vitally important.

Psychologist David Elkind, author of the insightful book *All Grown Up and No Place To Go*, identifies peers as one of the main causes of what he calls the "patchwork self" in teenagers. Because they are desiring acceptance from all the important people in their lives, teenagers don't have a strong sense of individual identity.

Instead, they develop this "patchwork self," a conglomeration of behaviors, attitudes, and even personality traits that will help them achieve acceptance from peers, teachers, parents, coaches, siblings, and other significant people in their lives.

If we are to be effective in meeting students' needs through our programs, we must do two things to address this powerful issue of peer acceptance. First, we must build our youth groups to have a strong sense of accepting fellowship so that students' strongest peer relationships can be built in a Christian environment. Second, we must engage in serious relationships with students so that we meet their peers and observe the influence that is present.

If I challenge my students about the dangers of being a "chameleon," always changing its colors to protect itself by adapting to the environment, they are sure to feel convicted about the negative influence of their peers, but they may feel powerless to change. It is only with strong support from me or other youth leaders that they are ever able to break away from their peers. If I am to be effective, I must realize the intense need my students have for their peers, and then I can challenge and direct them to keep their peer need under God's control.

4. *The church or youth group.* Understanding the contemporary world of the teenagers with whom we work does not always take place outside of the youth group. As a matter of fact, quite a lot can be learned through listening to and observing our own church kids.

I used to refuse students the right to bring their radios or tape decks on retreats. Now I allow it. Why? I guess I didn't want to fool myself into thinking that our religious students were more saintly than they were. When they brought their tapes, I found that they were just as secular as their peers, and often just as indiscriminate as to what they listened to.

If we are honest, we will find that our Christian students aren't all that different from their non-Christian peers. Our Christian students may not drink or take drugs, but many romanticize what it would be like to get drunk or high. They may be sexual virgins, but this may be more from lack of opportunity than from spiritual convictions.

We learn about the world of our youth group kids the same

way we learn about the school environment: we listen, hang around, and spend time with students. Sometimes I pretend to be the first one asleep in the cabin on a retreat just so that I can hear the conversations that go on "behind my back." I also enjoy the long rides to retreat locations or on mission teams because in these times students open up and tell me some of the deepest things about themselves.

Understanding the world within our youth groups requires some vulnerability on our part. First, it requires us to accept that many of our young people will be spiritual schizophrenics; they can talk about their devotion to the Lord in one breath and be telling their girlfriends that they are "hot-blooded" in the next.

Second, it requires us to recognize our own hypocrisies and the hypocrisies of the adults in our church (including some of the parents of the group members). If we are honest, we will see that teenagers are just like us, and seeing their spiritual shallowness will be a rebuke to our own.

5. *Their individual worlds.* The invention of the Walk-Man, the coming of cable television, and the rental of movies to be shown at home points to a basic desocialization occurring within our society. As a result, an increasing number of teenagers withdraw into themselves, making it almost impossible for parents and concerned adults to know what's going on inside them.

If the family and the school worlds are hard to enter, the individual, inner world of the teenager is almost impossible to penetrate. We can only surmise what's going on in there by external behaviors and self-revelation from the teenagers themselves.

In general, however, we can make some basic observations that can help us to understand and to meet the teenager's needs.

a. *Today's teenagers feel at odds with the world.* This is a general result of the artificial world of adolescence; students feel they don't belong to the world of children or to the world of the adult. Physically and socially they feel awkward, so again they retreat to the only people they think will understand: their peers. By themselves, they feel "embarrassed to be alive," as one writer put it.

b. *Today's teenagers feel unsure about themselves.* Teenagers have a special sense of insecurity because choices, the future, and the fear of failure loom over them like a guillotine about to drop. Their weak self-esteem makes them vulnerable to criticism, ridicule, and the fear of rejection.

c. *Today's teenagers want help but are often afraid to ask.* *Christianity Today* published an interview with youth experts entitled "The Myth of the Generation Gap." The experts made this point: students are more responsive to parents and adults than we usually give them credit for. There is something going on inside their heads, and one of those things is what Strommen calls a "cry" for help—"Help me understand myself, the world, and where I fit in."[3]

Understanding that there is a lot going on inside of our young people can help us probe more deeply to find out where their hurts are and how we can understand these needs. With this type of understanding in mind, our programs can be geared to greater effectiveness.

IDENTIFY, DON'T BECOME IDENTICAL

We try to understand our teenagers' worlds not to become like them but to address their needs more effectively. Pat Hurley warns us against adopting adolescent behavior: "Being 'real' in the youth culture does not mean trying to be a 'kid.' You are an adult who relates to the youth mindset. Being a free person, a person that they can trust, will provide an environment of spontaneity and flexibility wherever you go, whether it's a one-on-one appointment to get a Coke, a youth group meeting, or a Sunday school class."[4]

MORE TIPS FOR KEEPING FRESH

Understanding and responding to the teenage world takes work, as we have already observed. There are, however, some practical ways that we can learn about the youth culture in order to try to determine teenagers' needs.

Consider these tips:

---

[3] "The Myth of the Generation Gap," *Christianity Today* (Oct. 19, 1984).
[4] Pat Hurley, *The Penetrators*, (Wheaton, IL: Victor Books, 1978), 27.

- Listen to the radio stations your students listen to. Why do they listen? What makes certain disk jockeys more likeable than others? What are the words of the most popular songs saying about life? Love? Values?

- Watch the most popular TV shows. Why are they popular? What do students enjoy in them?

- See the current hit movies. Why are they teenage hits? Who are the heroes? What is the message?

- Read a book about adolescent development. Where do your students fit into the ideas of this book?

- Read a book about adolescent trends. Do you see these trends in the young people of your city or town? Why or why not?

- Read newsletters about youth events and trends. Ask if they apply to the young people you know (always be careful in responding to "trends"; remember that these newsletters are written *by* adults *for* adults, and students don't often reduce themselves to easily identifiable trends).

- Take a few formal or informal surveys. This can be done in a group or one-on-one. A survey also can be a series of questions that you ask students without ever asking them to record their answers.

- Talk to school teachers or administrators. What trends do they see? What needs are they confronting in the students of your community?

- Look over the school calendar. What events will attract the most students? Why?

- Find out who the most popular students are in school. Why are they popular? If there are no dominant popular students, what does this say about the sense of community at the school?

Understanding teenagers is a tough task, but some creative research into the worlds in which they live can help us understand their needs and address our youth ministries and programs to these needs.

8.
WORKING WITH
A TEAM

When the writer of the Book of Proverbs observed "many counselors bring success" (Prov. 15:22, TLB), he made a very important observation for effective, long-term youth ministry. We can't do it alone. The diversity of our students, the demands of leadership, and the need for quality one-on-one ministry forces us to build a team of associates who will lead the youth ministry with us.

Scripture exhorts us to realize the importance of teamwork. Consider the Old Testament example of Moses. With all of his responsibilities related to leading the people of Israel, he was overwhelmed. When his pagan father-in-law, Jethro, observed his counseling from sunup to sundown, Jethro made one basic observation: "You can't do it alone. The thing you are doing isn't good" (Exod. 18:18). Jethro knew that Moses was headed on a fast track to burnout. The remedy that Jethro taught was basic delegation—leadership through a group of associate leaders.

The New Testament's most powerful example of team leadership is Jesus with his twelve disciples. By spending a good portion of his active ministry training these men (most scholars estimate that he spent over fifty percent of his active ministry with just his chosen twelve), Jesus prepared them for the future preaching of the gospel. His example of discipleship was simple: I am going to train you so that you can carry out a broader and more extensive ministry than I could alone.

The model of Jesus overlaps the biblical teaching on spiritual gifts in 1 Corinthians 12. The body has many different members, all of whom are equipped with a variety of spiritual abilities so that the whole body can benefit. If we understand and believe in the body of Christ, we must acknowledge that there is no room for the "Lone-Ranger" mentality that kills leaders in youth ministry. We must work alongside others for the building up of the whole body of Christ.

When I first assumed youth ministry leadership, I entered with a self-centered and haughty attitude: "If you want something done right, do it yourself." My attitude was quickly changed as I got into the mainstream of the youth ministry. The teaching of Scripture changed my perspective theologically, but my personal helplessness changed my thinking practically. I realized that Jethro was right: I couldn't do it alone. The quantity and diversity of our students required me to recruit others to work alongside me. I needed other members of the body of Christ to complement and supplement my gifts and leadership.

The result was a team-oriented philosophy of ministry that has since undergirded everything that we have undertaken in the youth ministry. Simply stated, we arrived at the conclusion that the work of Christ must be done by a team of interdependent people. Such a team frees everyone to do a particular job to his or her fullest capability. We didn't need superstars; we needed each other.

CHOOSING A TEAM

The nature of youth work—diverse students, multiple needs, and broad-ranging responsibilities—demands a team, but whom do we recruit? A frequent frustration of many leaders is that those who are willing are often ill-equipped or wrongly motivated (like suspicious parents who want to join the staff team to keep an eye on their own children). On the other hand, the most capable people are people in demand; we may not be able to get them to join our ministry because they already are serving in a dozen other locations.

Nevertheless, we need a team. And we need to match volunteer leaders with the needs and opportunities of our ministries; the junior high staff leader may need more patience or different gifts from the leader of the college-age group. When matching people to needs, however, we must look for at least six basic qualities:

1. *Love for Christ.* In Luke's gospel, Jesus reminds us that a student, after he is fully trained, will become like his teacher (Luke 6:40). Our students will become like those whom we recruit to lead them. If we desire to produce students who love Jesus Christ, we had better recruit leaders with that same quality.

When I first met Ted, I said to myself, "Now here is a guy that I would like to recruit for our youth team." He was tall, handsome, successful, and popular. He had a solid testimony, and I would dream about the number of students he could influence for Christ. I recruited Ted, but I made a big mistake. He did have a great conversion testimony, but that was all. Ted loved Ted much more than he loved Jesus Christ, and he wanted the youth group members to love Ted almost as much as he did. He attracted students—the egocentric, the insecure, and the idol-worshipers— and I found myself wishing I knew how to fire him. I realized that I went after the wrong qualities, and I got burned in the process.

On the other hand, Betty was a wise recruit. She didn't have an overwhelming personality, but her primary strength was her love for the Lord. Her example enabled her to be one of the strongest disciplers in our ministry.

2. *Love for students.* Each of us will meet people who will be open to joining the youth team, but they will express their hesitancy after they start spending time with students. One person put it this way to me: "Paul, I love the Lord, and I know that he wants to reach these students, but these gum-smacking, hair-twisting, loud-mouthed ninth-grade girls are simply too much for me."

What she was saying was not a confession of some great sinful attitude. She was simply admitting that she was not quite ready to work with these students. She had a hard time loving them, and she knew that her performance would be affected.

Although "love for teenagers" isn't listed in any of the biblical lists of spiritual gifts, I do believe that it is a God-given ability. Actually, I believe that the *desire* to love teenagers is God-given, and when this desire is cultivated, we are able to pour ourselves into students who might drive other people crazy.

Love for students has made Walt a very effective member of our youth team. He isn't outspoken or necessarily good-looking, athletic, or popular. He just loves students. He goes out of his way to sit with them. He knows how to draw them out and get them to trust him. And Walt is a happily married father of two, so I know he isn't reaching out to teens because of some psychological need in himself. He genuinely loves teenagers, and he is a great example to the rest of our team.

3. *Willingness to grow.* The first two qualities might lead us to wonder if there is anyone who can qualify for the volunteer leadership team. Actually we can find many qualified people if we are willing to accept those who haven't arrived yet but are willing to grow.

In practical terms, I would rather recruit a young Christian who says "I want to grow in the Lord by serving others" than an older, more mature Christian who acts as if he or she has it all together. I would rather recruit someone who says, "I am not sure that I can love teenagers, but I am willing to work at it" than a person who acts as if he or she has all the answers for youth ministry.

We were approached once by a young couple who came to "offer their expertise in youth ministry." As we talked with them, they bragged about their years of involvement as youth sponsors at another church, their intense knowledge of youth culture, and their desire to help us in our ministry. I never found out whether or not they were experts. I thanked them and said, in effect, "Don't call us, we'll call you." Even if they were experts, their attitudes told me that they were not the type who would condescend to the rest of us so that we could grow alongside them.

4. *Willingness to make a commitment.* Although the longevity and endurance of the youth leader is important to the success of the youth ministry, the commitment of the lay leaders is likewise critical. Students take a long time to open up and to trust the adults who work with them, so high turnover in the volunteer team will hinder the ministry.

It's not unreasonable to require volunteers to commit at least one year to the youth ministry team. Those who commit themselves for a longer period will experience deeper and more significant results in the students they are working with.

People often are hesitant to make a commitment, especially to such an unknown commodity as youth. How can we help them? In our ministry, we recommend that people join the youth team for one month before making a full commitment. We have found that this enables people to observe the youth ministry without the pressure of a commitment.

Over the course of this month, our new recruits are placed with some seasoned veterans. This lets the new person see effectiveness in action, and it gives the new person the time to find out if he or she is qualified to work with teenagers. It also gives us the chance to see if the person falls into the "willing-but-not-able" category. At the end of the month, we decide. We have been blessed by God's leading. Each person who has made the commitment has met with the approval of the other staff. Each person who was considered unqualified for youth work has come to that conclusion before the staff has had to refuse him or her.

5. *Flexibility.* If people want us to predict exactly how teenagers will behave, perhaps they shouldn't join the youth team. People must be willing to understand that teenagers defy generalization, and as a result, teenagers are an enigma even to those who call themselves youth experts.

A healthy volunteer team is also flexible about the tasks assigned to them. A Sunday school teacher must at times be willing to take a pie in the face. The music leader must be willing to help with the administration of the retreat weekend or the formation of the youth budget. Recognizing our various spiritual gifts doesn't mean that we become such specialists that we refuse to serve where needed.

6. *A sense of humor.* If someone is going to join the youth team, he or she must be able to laugh, especially at himself or herself. Issues like baldness, fat stomachs, or physical shortcomings will cause joking among our image-conscious teenagers, and if we don't learn to laugh at ourselves, we surely will be hurt.

The dynamic of being able to laugh at oneself also will be needed in the process of growth on the team. When we work with other members of the volunteer team, we will learn much about ourselves. Our selfishness or stubbornness or pride will surface, and in healthy team situations, these weaknesses will be confronted. To achieve maximum growth, we must be willing to laugh at ourselves and say, "You are right; I am that way. Please help me change."

Laughter is also important because it provides an important bridge to our students. Laughter disarms people, and it relaxes us to relate to each other with greater openness. My friend Scott is a Hell's-Angels-type biker. One day he came into the church office with his all-black outfit and his bulging muscles rippling out of his sleeveless T-shirt, revealing his many tattoos. One of the secretaries stared quite conspicuously at him. The moment was tense until little four-year-old Aaron, the son of another minister, quipped, "Hey mister, why do you use crayons on your arms?" Everyone laughed. The tension was broken through humor.

BUILDING THE TEAM

Our youth ministry staff has adopted a motto about the growth on our volunteer junior high and senior high teams; we say, "A healthy staff team begets a healthy youth ministry." Leadership experts would call this the "trickle down" theory. If the leaders are growing and feel competent, the whole organization benefits.

This growth of the leadership team, however, doesn't come accidentally or automatically. It occurs when we as team leaders commit ourselves to building the team qualitatively and quantitatively.

Qualitative growth requires us to become trainers. Whatever we know about youth work must be imparted to others. We may not feel like experts, but we can at least stay one step ahead of our volunteer partners in ministry. Our co-workers will look to us for spiritual and ministry direction, and we must be ready to offer it.

Qualitative growth requires us to become disciplers. Time with our volunteer staff to insure their spiritual health or to encourage them in their ministry is time well spent for the benefit of the whole youth group.

Qualitative growth requires us to become nurturers. Like us, the volunteer team needs to grow as adults; they need to be wrestling with God at work in their own lives so that they can feel like healthy adults. If they feel content that they are growing, they will feel more equipped to give themselves away to the youth.

As leaders, we also must work for quantitative growth. Although the members on the team can help in contacting others, we still have the greater responsibility to act as recruiters. We have to work to see the team size increase. One leader for every six or eight students is ideal, although many youth groups are forced to get by with one leader to every ten or twelve.

Such quantitative growth will require us to plan ahead, get visibility at church or in other church groups from which volunteers may come, and share with others how they may be used in the ministry. Quantitative growth becomes simpler, however, if the qualitative growth is of a consistently high caliber. If the staff team is growing and dynamic, others will want to join in the effort for their own growth as well as for the ministry to the students.

PROBLEMS WITH TEAM MINISTRY

You often may feel that it is easier to do the work all alone rather than deal with the problems of working with a team.

1. *Conflicts within the teams.* One thing we can be sure of: every person who joins the youth leadership team will be a sinner, including us. As a result, we must carefully maintain relationships if the team is to stay healthy. If we are not careful, we may find that

- one staff member is particularly successful with his or her students and others who are struggling with their own small groups or in their leadership get jealous.

- romantic relationships arise between various members of the team, and those who are left out *feel* left out.

- staff members disagree with standards of discipline or they feel uncomfortable with the youth group's stance on issues like rock music or drinking or dancing.

- some staff members disagree with the group's goals; they may complain, "Why do we have to deal with all this 'caring-for-each-other' stuff; why can't we just get on with ministry to the kids?"
- staff members may pull practical jokes on each other and hurt one of the participants.

Conflicts do occur, and the only guaranteed way to avoid them is to dismantle the team. However, the better solution is to anticipate these conflicts before they occur. Talk to the volunteers about the conflicts, addressing them as a positive challenge for growth rather than a trap to avoid. When the conflicts do occur, address them directly with the team members involved. In my earliest youth ministry days, I used to think that problems would go away or that time would heal wounds. I learned that time infects wounds, and it is better to dress the wound early than to let it fester.

2. *Conflicts over use of time.* As soon as we recruit a team, we have two groups of people needing our time and attention: the youth and the leadership team. We will find ourselves faced with the perpetual question, "With whom do I spend my time? Which group is my priority?"

The answer is both. We need to invest ourselves in leaders so that they, in turn, can invest themselves in students, but we also need to spend good time with students so that we can develop our abilities to work with teenagers. Set aside regular time to invest in each group. Let your leadership team know that youth activities and youth retreats are student times; during these activities your priority is to minister to students. But also schedule staff retreats, monthly staff training days, and occasional staff socials to devote your full attention to the needs of your staff.

3. *Conflicts over authority.* When people join the leadership team, they automatically will be called upon to exercise some authority. It could be disciplining a student or answering questions related to a tough Scripture passage. Their age and position give them natural authority.

Conflicts emerge when co-workers differ over how the authority should be used. Some will want to give dogmatic answers to every tough question, while others may want to leave these questions unanswered. When discipline issues arise, staff—like parents—can differ on the degree or severity of the punishment.

As leaders, we must intervene in these situations, taking authority even over co-leaders. As team leaders, we will need to make the ultimate decisions, even when the team members don't agree with us unanimously.

4. *Conflicts about our perceived role.* As other team members assume visible roles, people from the church may question our leadership, wondering why *we* aren't up front all of the time. It's always easiest to be a one-person show, but visibility isn't our priority. We perhaps can avert some criticism by explaining the team ministry philosophy to the leaders to whom we report; if they understand what we are doing, they can defend us against criticism. (If they disagree with the team ministry concept, we may need to consider looking for a new job.)

A TALE OF YOUTH MINISTRY

Once upon a time, a talented young man came to the youth ministry of Amalgamated Community Church. He could sing, teach, lead games, and win students to Jesus Christ. The youth group at Amalgamated grew and grew, and the talented young man just kept on giving himself to his youth group. From morning to night he would counsel, plan, meet with students on campus, and call kids just to let them know he cared. (No one was quite sure if he was single or married, but most assumed that he was single because he never seemed to go home except to sleep.)

The young man's talents carried him for a long time, but he soon grew lonely. He spent all his time caring for students, but he began to wonder if anyone cared about him. But although he was discouraged, he kept on meeting with students, planning meetings, and scheduling activities.

Then one day a bratty junior high boy came to the talented young man. The talented young man knew that this bratty boy was not a Christian, but the boy came to youth activities and listened.

The bratty boy said to the talented young man, "In my advanced managerial training symposium for eighth graders, we are studying the principles of delegation, and it is statistically proven that executives who refuse to delegate dramatically increase the likelihood of their own attrition."

The talented young man didn't understand all these big words, so the bratty boy explained them to the young man: "You can't do it alone. If you teach mutual interdependence of the parts of the body of Christ, then why do you act alone all of the time? Are you the returned Christ? Or are you just ignorant of your need for others?"

The talented young man started to understand, but his face revealed that the bratty boy's ideas were still too complex. The bratty boy grew impatient: "In short . . . before you plan one more day in youth ministry, get some people to help you!"

Finally the talented young man understood, and he began to recruit a team. The team included an intelligent man who reached out to the bratty boy. As the relationship between the intelligent man and the bratty boy grew, the bratty boy became a Christian. When he was a man, he became the executive director of the Amalgamated Community Church Management Workshop.

The talented young man became a talented old man, but he served the youth ministry at Amalgamated Community Church for forty years because of the effective team that worked with him. He even worked with the bratty young son of the executive director of the Church Management Workshop, but he did it through his youth leadership team.

And they all lived happily ever after.

9.
DETERMINING THE SPIRITUAL CLIMATE

If our only goal in youth ministry is good programming, we should send our young people to school activities, Boys' Clubs, or the YWCA. But our goals go beyond programs and activities. Our primary goal is spiritual; we want to see young people come to know Jesus Christ, grow in their faith, be able to articulate their faith to others, and approach adulthood with a realistic and working relationship with God.

This is a high calling!

"We proclaim Him [Christ], admonishing every man and teaching every man with all wisdom, that we may present every man *complete* in Christ" (Col. 1:28 NASB, italics added). This completeness in Christ will not be achieved by the time our students reach age eighteen, but they can be moving toward such completeness.

Too many youth leaders underestimate the potential of teenagers. We often think, "If only we can hold on to them until they go through adolescence, maybe then they can make effective commitments for Christ." We think that teenagers are superficial or spiritually dead, so we program to that end and thus fulfill our own predictions. One cartoon showed a youth minister dressed up like a clown getting ready for the weekly fun-and-games youth activity. A junior high boy approached him, saying, "I'm deeply concerned over the hunger crisis in Africa." Teenagers think on a deeper level than we sometimes give them credit for.

Effective youth ministry planning and organization is built on a spiritual foundation. Through all of our efforts—Sunday school lessons, fun activities, retreats, choirs, service projects—we should be building for maximum spiritual growth in our young people.

But how?

WHAT IS OUR SPIRITUAL CLIMATE?

Conversations with dozens of youth leaders across the country have taught me that every youth group is different. The spiritual climate differs in each church or group. Thus a uniform "Spiritual Growth Program" is artificial or ineffective.

Our teenagers, for example, generally come from Christian homes. The students who aren't from Christian homes are from "moral" homes (so we have to be careful not to equate Christian faith with doing good things). Most of the students live with both parents (although single-parent families are becoming more common), and students have a positive feeling toward church (or, at least, toward religion).

Other youth ministers I have met have much different spiritual climates. Broken homes are the norm, not the exception. Positive feelings toward church exist only on Christmas. Religious teaching in the home is rare. Few, if any, of the students profess a personal faith in Christ, and those that do have little understanding of living in obedience to the Bible.

Building a youth program without understanding the spiritual climate leads to disaster. Understanding the spiritual climate is never easy, but we can look at five areas to help us understand our students' spiritual awareness:

1. *Our church or youth group.* Youth-group history, overall church programs, and spiritual leadership (if any) will tell us something about the spiritual health of our group. One friend took over a youth group that had never had a Bible study. Most of the students were not Christians, but they loved the youth group because it gave them a sense of belonging to a group.

When the youth leader started working with students one-on-one, leading some to faith in Christ, trouble started. The spiritual dynamic changed in the youth group, but the social climate also changed: suddenly there was an "in" group (those who had come to faith) and an "out" group (those who were still undecided).

To maintain spiritual growth in this situation, the youth leader worked diplomatically, reconciling friends to friends and students to parents. The spiritual climate and history of the youth group made his job all the more difficult.

The spiritual climate of the church is also very important. If the youth leader is told that his or her purpose is to "keep the kids in the church," then there may be trouble ahead. Many youth leaders have struggled greatly as they challenged young people to grow in their faith, only to find that the parents are put on the defensive. "We wanted you to keep them in the church, not make them into 'Jesus freaks,'" was the comment one zealous youth leader got from a church leader. If the adults at the church are growing, it will be a lot easier to stimulate similar growth in the youth group.

2. The families. Jimmy came from a troubled family. He coped with his own troubles by getting high almost every day. His school work suffered, and his life was in a shambles. When he went away to summer camp, he was transformed by the power of Christ. He was delivered from his drug habit, restored to a new sense of purpose, and reconciled to God, giving him a great sense of peace. When the testifying, Bible-reading, transformed Jimmy came home, his mother was amazed, then furious.

She came to me with the most hostile words I have heard in youth ministry: "What have you done to my son? I would rather see him back on drugs than into all this Jesus stuff!"

When our teenagers' families hold to such distorted values, any spiritual growth will be challenged severely. Jimmy's mother's case is unusual, but anger like this may surface if parents aren't growing in their own relationship with God. Students who are spiritually alive may put their parents on the defensive.

The spiritual climate at home is very influential on our youth ministries. If we are to help young people grow in their spiritual lives, we can't ignore the messages they hear from their parents. We must identify when we can build on the values and attitudes taught by the parents, and we must realize that sometimes we will be working in contrast to the spiritual climate at home.

3. *The students themselves.* The best way to find out what students think about God, spirituality, or obeying the Bible is to build our relationships with them. A one-time conversation will not yield much, except from students who are outspoken or articulate. For most of our students, we have to spend one-on-one time with them so that they will tell us what they are really feeling, not just what they think we want to hear.

This one-on-one research will give us information we never would learn in a large-group setting. Students going through deep questions may not feel free to discuss them in a large group. Similarly, students searching for a relationship with God may never express this in a group meeting. A one-on-one meeting may be the only place they feel safe to reveal their questions and doubts.

In our individual meetings with students, we may discover issues that we can effectively address in group meetings. Several years ago I realized that most of our students had Christian convictions about sexual morality, but few of them understood why they believed certain principles. Their spiritual need was to know the Bible's teaching on the subject. They knew what their church taught and what their parents thought, but if they were going to make those convictions their own, they needed to know what God commanded. We scheduled several seminars to discuss the Bible's view of sexual morality.

4. *The school or community.* Is there anything spiritual going on at school? What is the religious stance of the community? Answers to these questions can help us determine spiritual needs that our youth ministry program should address.

Over the course of the past ten years, I have found that religious conflict on local campuses has created opportunity for discussion about the gospel. The activity of local cult groups has created a heightened awareness of spiritual issues, and we have been able to build on this. At the peak of one cult's efforts on the high school campus, a local youth group sponsored a night with a woman who had been delivered from the cult after she had become a Christian. Hundreds of students attended that meeting.

Another reality that can cause an increase in spiritual discussion on the high school or junior high campus is death. The death of a teacher, a car accident in which several students are killed, or a student suicide all can serve to increase the sense of spiritual need. When we see these things happening, we can respond through our youth programs.

The religious attitudes in the community also can affect the spiritual climate of our youth groups. The people in our town are religious, but many believe that they will be saved by living a good life. Thus, the work projects our group does in the community are applauded and may increase attendance at our group, but unless we articulate our belief in salvation through faith alone, we often are perceived as believing that these work projects somehow make us right with God.

In more secularized communities, the challenges may be different. Attempts at leading students to faith in Christ may be seen as "cultic manipulation" (especially if students are converted on retreats where we have removed students from their homes, "deprived" them of sleep, and fed them starchy foods!). We may be seen as the cultic leaders, and students from our groups may be discredited at school or in the community.

In the typical community, however, such open hostility is rare. But we still should be aware that our students operate within the framework of school and community values, and our attempts at spiritual growth with our programs must be designed in the context of these other dynamics.

5. *Society.* The spiritual (or unspiritual) atmosphere of our society also affects our students. Television, videos, trends, movies, and fads all reflect the spiritual values that influence our students. If people sleep together outside of marriage in the teen-genre films, our youth will need to be convinced from God's perspective why this is wrong. If advertising is convincing teenagers that they are worthless individuals unless they are wearing the newest designer jeans or shirts, we'll have to work hard to communicate God's unconditional acceptance of them.

SPIRITUAL ISSUES

Whether or not students are open to spiritual discussion, some issues need to be addressed from a spiritual perspective. The themes behind these issues are timeless, but the way that we address them is very time dated. Thus, our challenge is to be *relevant*. When students hear discussions about issues that are of great concern to them, they are more open to hearing God's answers.

Ten issues that warrant discussion with any youth group include

1. *Self-image*. Who am I? In our society, our identity is increasingly based on externals: looks, clothing, accomplishments, grades, etc. Nowhere is this more true than the world of the teenager. The thought that "God accepts me just the way I am" is so revolutionary to most teenagers that we need to remind them of it repeatedly.

2. *Sexuality*. What does it mean to be a man or woman? If we confine our youth ministry lessons to how far teenagers should go in dating relationships, our students still will be ill-equipped to face society's stereotypes. We need to go further in our discussions and explain how sexuality and personhood are related. The great lie of the movies is that sex and self can be separated. Our students need to see from God's perspective that our sexuality can't be sacrificed without harming our entire personalities.

3. *Human worth*. What am I worth? Perhaps the greatest motivator toward teen suicide is the feeling of worthlessness. Media violence reflects this; families may reinforce this; predictions of future nuclear disaster may further stimulate this thought. If we are to make a dent in the thinking of the average teenager about his or her own self-worth before God, we must speak loudly against the shouts of our culture.

4. *Authority*. Who's in charge? Frank Sinatra's song "I Did It My Way" expresses the philosophy of many young people. If we are to communicate an honest faith to them, we must reverse this thinking by reminding them that human beings are not the measure of all things. We are accountable to a higher authority— God.

5. *Truth/Fantasy*. What can I believe? Years ago experts estimated that a generation of children brought up on television will have seen over 15,000 hours of TV by the time they were sixteen years old. That generation is here, and they are confused about what is truth. They have watched hundreds of murderers who experience no punishment or guilt; they have seen thousands of adulterers who experience no remorse or pain in their relationships. Yet we say that God's ways are true and right. The distinction between truth and unreality isn't too clear to our students: is believing in Jesus the same to them as believing in Conan the Barbarian? Any presentation of spiritual truth makes our reliance on the Holy Spirit absolutely necessary because we are teaching students for whom truth is sometimes very fuzzy.

6. *Escapism*. Where can I go when I am in pain? We need to communicate to today's young people that our God is a refuge and strength, a help in the time of need. When teenagers are tempted to withdraw into drugs, alcohol, or fantasy, we must be able to point them to the God who knows their pain and who can comfort them. Through our teaching and the example of our own turning to God in the midst of pain, we can encourage our students to find peace in their relationship to God.

7. *Family breakdown*. What is a normal family? Today's families are under great stress. Relationships and family structures based on God-given standards are the exception rather than the rule. Effective spiritual teaching with our young people should incorporate sensitive instruction on *coping* (how to make the best of the present situation) as well as *relating* (developing healthy relationships that will become the prototypes of future families).

8. *Sovereignty of God*. Can God handle it? Do our students believe, like Rabbi Kushner in his *Why Bad Things Happen to Good People*, that bad things happen to good people because God is impotent to stop the bad things? In our efforts to answer the spiritual questions of our young people, we can't shy away from the tough questions. First, we need to wrestle with our own faith, and then we can communicate our answers to our students. They need to know—especially in the midst of their changing lives—that God

is sovereign, that no challenge is too difficult for him, and that he will bring about his divine purposes.

9. *Mind control.* What's the use of thinking for myself? Many forces contend for the control of our students' minds: cult groups, TV, and even their parents. Many young people don't want to think for themselves. The world isn't an easy place to figure out, especially when you are young. But promoting responsible spiritual growth in our teenagers will force us to challenge them to think for themselves. In John Milton Gregory's *Seven Laws of Teaching*, he reminds us that a truth is learned only after we can articulate it for ourselves. In issues of faith and practice, we must teach students to ask their own questions, find the answers, and articulate the truths of the Christian life for themselves.

10. *Sin.* What's right and wrong? The word "sin" has become *passé.* We talk about problems that are culturally determined or errant behaviors that are environmentally reinforced, but we prefer not to talk about sin. Sin assumes an absolute right versus wrong, good versus evil. Yet, as Christians, we believe in sin. We believe in the Ten Commandments and the Sermon on the Mount. We believe that God does hold to absolutes by which we'll be judged, and our teaching to our youth groups should reflect this. In our efforts to be open to ideas of situational ethics, we must not follow our culture's relativistic teachings that render almost nothing absolute.

In the course of our youth ministry programming, these and other spiritual issues must be addressed, but they must be addressed in terms that students understand and with illustrations that are relevant to teen culture. If we do this, we will stimulate the spiritual climate because students will grow to see that the Bible is practical and that God is intimately concerned about the issues that bother them.

AN EXAMPLE

Last fall, we wanted to begin our program by finding out what the spiritual climate was in our youth group by taking a survey. We targeted our Sunday school class, our largest group, representing

the broadest cross section of our youth ministry. We asked three
questions:
1. What questions do you have about God?
2. What questions do you have about the Christian life?
3. What questions do you have about telling others about
   Christian faith?

The answers were broad and varied. Some were humorous,
others quite serious. Look them over and ask yourself how you
would design programs to address these questions.

1. *What questions do you have about God?*

- Why does God allow suffering/evil? (appeared multiple
  times)
- What is the Holy Spirit?
- Are we in the end times? (multiple)
- How can I be sure that Christianity is right?
- Can I be sure I am a Christian? (multiple)
- What about Creation and Evolution?

2. *What questions to you have about the Christian life?*

- How can I stop gossiping? (multiple)
- How can I love everybody? (multiple)
- Should I go to a Christian college?
- Can we make church services more interesting?
- How can I stop swearing? (multiple)
- How can I lead a Christian life in times of stress? (multiple)
- How can we make an uninteresting message interesting?
  (multiple)
- Should a Christian listen to rock music?
- Should boys wear tight pants?
- How can I deal with loneliness? Anger? Depression?
- How can I confront lukewarm Christianity? (multiple)
- How can I relate to my parents? (multiple)

- How can I deal with divorce?
- Should a Christian date a non-Christian? (multiple)
- What is life after death like? (multiple)

3. *What questions do you have about telling others about Christian faith?*

- How can I witness to family members? (multiple)
- How can I witness to someone from an Eastern religion?
- How can I witness without using clichés?
- How can I make better friends with non-Christians? (multiple)

CONCLUSION

Determining the spiritual climate will help us to increase our effectiveness in planning programs and teaching lessons that reflect an understanding of where our group members are in their relationships with God. When we do this, our students will begin to see that faith is relevant to their daily lives.

Remember, however, that the best way to determine this spiritual climate is personal relationships with students. Robert Coleman illustrates this need to build relationships in his example of Jesus with his twelve disciples:

> He *ate* with them, *slept* with them, and *talked* with them for the most part of His entire active ministry. They *walked* together along the lonely roads; they *visited* together in the crowded cities; they *sailed* and *fished* together in the Sea of Galilee; they *prayed* together in the deserts and in the mountains; and they *worshipped* together in the Synagogues and in the Temple.[5]

If Jesus involved himself this intensely in knowing his disciples, how much more we'll need to spend time with and know our students so that we—like Jesus—may address the Word of God to their lives and needs.

---

[5] Robert Coleman, *The Master Plan of Evangelism*, (Old Tappan, NJ: Revell, 1964), 43.

10.
WHAT DO WE DO WITH PARENTS?

If we could enter the minds of many youth workers, we often would find negative feelings toward parents. I know. I've had some of these feelings myself, and I have seen them in other youth leaders.

The negative attitudes, however, aren't always obvious. Sometimes they surface through our jokes or our sarcastic remarks about parents. Other times our negative feelings arise out of a genuine hurt caused by a parent's painful criticism. In general, though, the negative feelings do come in certain distinguishable categories:

1. *Fear*. I feel fear when I see the father of a student walking toward me on the Sunday morning after one of our all-nighters. I am afraid that his daughter has contracted mononucleosis; I'm afraid that his son sneaked out during the night without my knowledge.

Fear of parents comes from a variety of sources. It could be a result of our own youthfulness. It could be caused by negative experiences in the past—either the attack of a parent or a blunder on our part. Whatever the cause, we grow fearful of that parental call or letter or confrontation because we feel that every encounter questions our personal worth and puts our jobs at stake.

2. *Criticism*. Perhaps it's just a reaction to our fears, or perhaps it's caused by our observations of some parents' failure with their children. Whatever the cause, we in youth group leadership sometimes engage in severe criticism of parents. It might emerge

directly in a challenge to our youth (by exhorting them not to be hypocrites like their parents) or it might manifest itself indirectly through defensiveness whenever a parent approaches us.

3. *Pride*. Perhaps we are negative toward the parents of our youth group members because those parents are willing to question us. They ask if an "all-nighter" is really wise the night before final exams; they remind us of the shortcomings of our ministries. And our self-protecting pride makes us want to fight back. When they question our leadership, they question our worth, our accomplishments, our training, and our very being—or so we think.

4. *Apathy*. Perhaps the most dangerous negative attitude we can hold toward parents is apathy. We often think that parents are so out of touch with youth culture that they couldn't offer anything worth hearing. We fail to see them as important in our work with their children.

These negative attitudes seriously impair our ministries. Instead of exerting our efforts to defend ourselves to parents, we need to learn how to minister to and listen to them. They have much to teach us.

A NEW PERSPECTIVE ON PARENTS

Growing out of my own negative attitudes has taken time and some disciplined thinking, but it has begun. It has happened through changing and enlarging my perspectives on parents and my youth ministry. I have developed five perspectives that have helped me grow:

1. *The realistic perspective*. This perspective might not have occurred had I not stayed at the same church for ten years. Over time, I had the opportunity to see students grow up, graduate, go to college, start careers, and get married. I saw clearly that many of our young people turned out to be just like their parents. For good or for ill, their values, beliefs, attitudes, and commitments were remarkably similar to those of their parents.

This observation caused me to rethink my youth ministry. I began to get the real picture: If I am going to have a substantial, long-term effect on the youth, I have got to try to affect the parents as well.

In practice, this has meant that I must challenge parents to spiritual commitment and to deeper personal faith—even as I challenge their children. If I want our students to be generous, I must be willing to encourage the parents to be the same. Youth ministry without attention to the long-term parental effect can yield only short-term, shallow results.

2. *The biblical perspective.* Paul's directive to parents and children in Ephesians 6 is clear: Parents hold the ultimate responsibility for raising their children. With this biblical perspective in mind, the place of the youth ministry changes. No longer do we need to hold ourselves responsible or guilty for each rebellious teenager in the church. Rather we can see ourselves as supporting parents. We should be asking them, "How can I assist you in your ministry with your children?" While the strategic importance of youth ministry doesn't diminish, our sense of ultimate responsibility for the young people does.

Gaining this biblical perspective has helped me not only to relax and feel more comfortable as an assistant to parents but also to empathize with parents and to be more supportive of them.

3. *The professional perspective.* Over the years I have learned that many veteran youth workers were building *ministry to parents* into their youth ministry. Some were counseling parents; others were producing resource newsletters for parents; still others were themselves parents of teenagers. Some were reaching parents through seminars that prepared them to parent adolescents and through ongoing parent support groups. Others were just recommending resource books to parents. But most of the youth groups that are serious about a long-term impact on the lives of youth are ministering to parents as well.

4. *The parental perspective.* In the course of having my attitude changed toward parents, the realistic perspective appealed to my practical nature ("It's necessary"), the biblical perspective appealed to my theology ("This is the way that God wants it"), and the professional perspective appealed to my desire to be current ("Everyone else seems to be going this way"). The parental perspective, however, appealed to my compassion.

Reading books like *Parents in Pain* by John White (InterVarsity Press) and *The Hurting Parent* by Margie Lewis (Zondervan), counseling parents who were heartbroken over their children's bad decisions, and watching the pain that many teenagers caused their parents, I began to see the parents of our youth as those who needed support, who wanted whatever help I could offer, and who desperately wanted to do the right thing for their children. I came to realize that their criticisms or harsh remarks toward me often were a cry for help and a projection of their own feelings of failure. I realized that many parents are deeply concerned about their children and are interested in knowing about the teenage world, the pressures their children face, and the resources available through the youth group. Seeing things from the parents' perspective helped me to see them as allies in the youth ministry rather than as adversaries.

5. *The practical perspective*. The utilitarian attitude of "If it works, do it" can be dangerous, but this pragmatic approach has helped change my negative attitudes toward parents. Put simply, I have found that cooperating with parents *works*. Parents are more supportive when I communicate to them what I am trying to do. They are ready to share (and be appreciative) when they realize that I care about the growth of their young people and not just the success of the youth group.

In the course of changed thinking about parents, I have added parents on our volunteer staff. At first this threatened me, but now I see it as a great asset. They bring the wisdom and compassion of parenthood to our youth team. They are the best resources for counseling the troubled parent, and they provide excellent role models for the students who have no healthy parental models at home. They also have changed me. They have changed my negative, defensive attitude into one of trust and respect.

As we allow our perspectives to be broadened, we will see the need to include parents in our planning for the youth ministry. If we see them as co-workers in our ministries and ourselves as co-workers in theirs, the overall ministry of reaching and discipling their children will be broadened, and our effectiveness will be increased.

Resources for Part II

VOLUNTEERS

Ammons, Edsel Albert. *Voluntarism and the Church.* Evanston, Illinois: Bureau of Social and Religious Research, 1976.

Christie, Les. *Unsung Heroes.* Grand Rapids: Zondervan, 1987.

Concklin, Robert. *How To Get People To Do Things.* Chicago: Contemporary, 1979.

Hagstrom, Richard. *Getting Along With Yourself and Others.* Wheaton, Illinois: Tyndale House Publishers, Inc., 1981.

Haines, Michael. *Volunteers: How To Find Them, How To Keep Them.* Vancouver, B.C.: Voluntary Action Resources Center, 1977.

Holderness, Ginny. *Youth Ministry—The New Team Approach.* Atlanta, Georgia: John Knox, 1981.

Johnson, Douglas W. *The Care and Feeding of Volunteers.* Nashville, Tennessee: Abingdon Press, 1978.

McDounough, Reginald M. *Working With Volunteer Leaders in the Church.* Nashville, Tennessee: Broadman, 1976.

Menking, Stanley J. *Helping Laity Help Others.* Philadelphia: Westminster Press, 1985.

Naylor, Harriet H. *Volunteers Today—Finding, Training and Working With Them.* New York: Association Press, 1967.

Pell, Arthur R. *Recruiting, Training, and Motivating Volunteer Workers.* New York: Pilot, 1977.

Releasing the Potential of the Older Volunteer. Los Angeles: Ethel Percy, Andrus Gerontology Center, 1976.

Schindler-Rainman, Eva. *The Volunteer Community.* Washington: Center For a Voluntary Society, 1971.

Senter, Mark. *The Art of Recruiting Volunteers.* Wheaton, Illinois: Victor Books, 1984.

Stone, J. David, and Miller, Rose Mary. *Volunteer Youth Workers.* Loveland, Colorado: Group Books, 1985.

Willey, Ray (ed.). *Working with Youth: A Handbook for the Eighties.* Wheaton, Illinois: Victor Books, 1982.

DETERMINING STUDENT NEEDS

Elkind, David. *All Grown Up and No Place To Go.* Reading, Massachusetts: Addison-Wesley, 1984.

Norman, Jane, and Harris, Myron L. *The Private Life of the American Teenager.* New York: Rawson Wade Publishers, 1981.

Strommen, Merton P. *Five Cries of Youth.* New York: Harper & Row, 1974.

Williams, Dick. *A Guide for Discipling Youth.* Glendale, California: Gospel Light, 1977.

MINISTRY TO PARENTS AND FAMILIES

Adams, Jay E. *Christian Counselors Manual.* Grand Rapids: Baker, 1973.

Borthwick, Paul. *But You Don't Understand.* Nashville, Tennessee: Thomas Nelson, 1986.

Buntman, Peter H., and Saris, E. M. *How To Live With Your Teenagers.* Pasadena, California: Birch Tree Press, 1982.

Bustanoby, Andre. *But I Didn't Want a Divorce.* Grand Rapids: Zondervan Publishing House, 1978.

Campbell, Ross. *How To Really Love Your Teenager.* Wheaton, Illinois: Victor Books, 1981.

Collins, Gary R. *Christian Counseling: A Comprehensive Guide.* Waco, Texas: Word Books, 1980.

Davitz, Lois, and Davitz, Joel. *How To Live (Almost) Happily With a Teenager.* Minneapolis, Minnesota: Winston Press, 1982.

DiGiacomo, James, and Wakin, Edward. *Understanding Teenagers: A Guide for Parents.* Allen, Texas: Argus Books, 1983.

Dobson, James. *Dr. Dobson Answers Your Questions.* Waco, Texas: Word Books, 1983.

_____. *Preparing For Adolescence.* Waco, Texas: Word Books, 1980.

Farel, Anita M. *Early Adolescence: What Parents Need To Know.* Carrboro, North Carolina: Center for Early Adolescence, n.d.

Hart, Archibald D. *Children and Divorce.* Waco, Texas: Word Books, 1985.

Johnson, Rex. *Communication: Key to Your Parents.* Irvine, California: Harvest House, 1978.

Kesler, Jay. *Let's Succeed With Our Teenagers.* Elgin, Illinois: David C. Cook, 1973.

Kesler, Jay (ed.). *Parents and Teenagers*. Wheaton, Illinois: Victor Books, 1984.

Kolb, Erwin J. *Parents' Guide to Conversations About Sex*. St. Louis: Concordia Press, 1980.

Lewis, Margie. *The Hurting Parent*. Grand Rapids: Zondervan Publishing House, 1980.

Narramore, Bruce. *Help! I'm a Parent!* Grand Rapids: Zondervan Publishing House, 1972.

Perez, Joseph F. *Family Counseling: Theory and Practice*. New York: D. Van Nostrand, 1979.

Ridenour, Fritz. *What Teenagers Wish Their Parents Knew About Kids*. Waco, Texas: Word Books, 1983.

Rinehart, Stacy, and Rinehart, Paula. *Choices: Finding God's Way in Dating, Sex, and Marriage*. Colorado Springs, Colorado: NavPress, 1984.

Sell, Charles M. *Family Ministry*. Grand Rapids: Zondervan Publishing House, 1981.

Skoglund, Elizabeth. *Coping*. Ventura, California: Regal Books, 1980.

Stafford, Tim. *The Trouble With Parents*. Wheaton, Illinois: Campus Life Books, 1978.

Strommen, Merton P., and Irene, A. *Five Cries of Parents*. New York: Harper & Row, 1984.

Wakefield, Norm. *You Can Have a Happier Family*. Ventura, California: Regal Books, 1977.

Wells, Joel. *How To Survive With Your Teenager*. Chicago: Thomas Moore Press, 1982.

White, John. *Parents in Pain*. Downers Grove, Illinois: InterVarsity Press, 1979.

Wilkerson, Rich. *Hold Me While You Let Me Go*. Eugene, Oregon: Harvest House, 1979.

Wilson, Earl D. *You Try Being a Teenager: To Parents To Stay in Touch*. Portland, Oregon: Multnomah Press, 1982.

Wright, Norman, and Johnson, Rex. *Communication: Key to Your Teenagers*. Irvine, California: Harvest House, 1978.

Ziglar, Zig. *Raising Positive Kids in a Negative World*. Nashville, Tennessee: Thomas Nelson, 1985.

Part III

ORGANIZING
YOUTH MINISTRY—
"NUTS AND BOLTS"

We all remember attending seminars that have stimulated us to implement a new idea or goal. We leave the seminar with zeal and determination only to find our excitement waning as we face the administrative details and day-to-day responsibilities of putting our good ideas and goals into practice. We remember getting bogged down with the "nuts and bolts" of the project, and some of us even abandoned our project because we became so discouraged by the logistical details.

The next chapters offer suggestions that may keep you from getting bogged down. These suggestions are designed to help you *improve your programs* and *delegate responsibilities*. I hope that these suggestions also will help you to think in a more organized way. Knowing what needs to be done and breaking the work load into manageable assignments is a large part of the administrative battle.

Rather than seeing organizational details as enemies, we must come to see them as tools that can serve us in our ministries. Rather than see planning and organizing as a waste of time, we must come to see them as essential to exercising our full potential. Even Jesus, the skilled master teacher, recognized the need for deliberate, organized plans as A. B. Bruce's classic *The Training of the Twelve* and Robert Coleman's *The Master Plan of Evangelism* both observe. If Jesus needed to plan and organize, then we need to do the same.

11.
DESIGNING AN EFFECTIVE YOUTH MINISTRY BUDGET

I gathered my student leaders together for a vision-and-planning meeting for our youth ministry. I came late, and found them in full discussion. They already had several hot ideas cooking: a river-rafting trip, a "super" concert with two or three top Christian musicians, and a gala retreat to Colorado. The room was buzzing with excitement.

As they reviewed their ideas with me, I tried to join in their enthusiasm, but my facial expressions gave away my inner tensions. "What's wrong?" asked one student. "Don't you like our ideas?"

"The ideas are great," I said, "but how much will all this cost? Where's the money going to come from?"

The buzzing stopped. No one had given much thought to money. "We were sorta hoping," muttered one student, "that the church would pay for it."

WHERE WILL THE MONEY COME FROM?

The question of cost has flattened creative planning and discouraged many youth groups from starting anything new. Our heightened awareness of expenses and the cost of living, combined with the trends toward decreased giving and a "let's-tighten-our-belts" attitude in churches and organizations, can be discouraging to youth workers.

And no wonder. With Christian concerts costing $10 to $12 per person, retreat weekends at $45 or more per person, and film rentals at a minimum of $50 each, the financial picture for a youth group can be bleak. When the normal costs of youth ministry programs (refreshments, speakers, films, etc.) are combined with extraordinary costs (special functions, emergency needs), the youth leader is left flustered and dismayed. Where *will* the money come from? How much *will* it cost?

Although Christian organizations and churches will vary widely in the amount of money available and the methods for allocating funds, an effective youth ministry budget is one of the best possible answers to the financial dilemmas and tensions in the youth program. How can such a budget be started or improved? The "youthfulness" of many of us in youth ministry leadership often means that we have little or no training or experience in administration. We need help.

FOUR BUDGET QUESTIONS TO GET US STARTED

We need to ask ourselves four critical questions as we begin our budget planning. The answers to these questions should help direct our efforts to be more effective in our management of money.

1. *What is the budget history of our church?* Explore the history of the youth ministry in which we are serving.

a. What has the youth ministry budget been in the past? $100? $1,000? Knowing this past amount will help us modify our dreams and expectations. A newly appointed seminary graduate may have 1,001 new ideas for the youth group, but he or she may be dismayed after presenting a budget in a church where nothing has been spent in the past on the youth ministry. The response may be, "We are already sticking our necks out by hiring and paying you, and now you want *more* money?"

b. What has the youth budget covered in the past? Sunday school curricula? Guest speakers? Refreshments? A youth worker who discovers that the youth budget is $12,000 may get very excited—until he or she finds out that this covers his or her salary, youth mailing, two retreats, and other ministry-related expenses.

c. Who controls the youth budget? An elder? The senior pastor? A parent? The youth minister? When the youth ministry budget is controlled by someone outside the youth ministry (or by someone who has a hidden agenda for the youth ministry), there may be some hidden costs in the budget. If we want to show a film to the group, do we need to get clearance from the entire board of deacons? Will we find ourselves spending money only to have the budget controller tell us that the budget won't cover such an item? Discovering the red tape associated with the budget may not save us any frustration, but it will at least help us be prepared for budget-related tensions.

Knowing the history of the youth ministry budget will enable us to plan with realistic expectations and awareness of our constraints.

2. *When should I begin to plan?* One day in May I received a call from a colleague. "Paul, we're starting to plan our summer program. Do you have any ideas you think could help us?" He was starting to plan for the summer—four weeks before the summer began!

Lack of planning or poor planning hampers many youth workers in creating summer programs or budgets. A few weeks before Jim's supervisor needed his proposed youth minstry budget for the next year, he reminded himself to set aside some time to think about the budget. Then he got involved in planning the Friday-night meeting, and one of the students had a crisis. Then at ten o'clock on the night before the budget was due, Jim remembered he hadn't even begun the final statement. He jotted some figures on a memo pad and handed them in.

If you've experienced a similar situation, then perhaps some suggestions will help you prepare next year's budget.

a. Maintain an ongoing file for ideas or needs that should be put into the next year's budget. The money we needed to fix a tire on the August bike trip is hard to remember when we establish the budget in January. When you return from the bike trip, write down your idea and throw it into the file.

b. Review your budget two or three months before the budget proposal is due. Use a checklist like this one to review the youth budget:

What will our expenses be for:

____ Educational resources

____ Capital equipment (overhead projectors, etc.)

____ Rental

____ Purchase

____ Bus or vehicle rental

____ Mission trip expenses

____ Honorariums for speakers/musicians

____ Film rental

____ Subsidies or scholarships for retreats

____ Gifts or prizes

____ Refreshments

____ Advertising and youth group mailings

____ Musical supplies/songbooks

____ Mileage reimbursement (for leaders who drive)

____ Decorations or holiday-related supplies

____ Athletic equipment

____ Film development for youth group use

____ Miscellaneous contingency fund

c. Break down the budget by month. This helps the treasurer anticipate cash flow and helps the youth leader envision a basic outline of the program.

d. After deciding on the approximate amount of money needed for the next year, *prioritize!* It's unrealistic to assume that the church leadership will rubber stamp whatever budget is proposed. If our budget-review committee comes back me with a request that we cut our budget by twenty percent, we need to know the essential and the nonessential items. Prioritizing the budget will enable us to make our own cuts according to ministry goals, which is much better than having an uninvolved committee cut our budgets randomly.

e. Decide how our budgeted monies will be accounted for. Will a youth group treasurer manage the checking account? Will all money need to go through the church treasurer? Planning ahead for proper management of the funds can save hundreds of headaches later.

3. *What are alternative means of financing?* The financial stresses of our age require that we be flexible and innovative in financing our youth group activities and needs. Consider these six ideas for paying for the program in ways other than a conventional budget.

a. *Let the students pay for themselves.* Statistics show that students on the high school campus today have twenty dollars per week (or more) discretionary spending money. Sadly enough, students are seldom challenged to spend their personal money on service to God or even on fun activities at the church. They spend it on themselves.

Challenging students to pay for themselves doesn't mean we make them pay for everything, but students should be allowed to "own" their own program by being involved financially. When students are responsible to raise their own money for an activity, they have an opportunity to see the power of God at work in people's lives. Students pay hundreds of their own dollars each year in our youth group for the opportunity to work in some missions setting. When people are astounded that our students *pay* for the chance to *work*, our young people are able to share about how God provided for them in some unusual ways. In our materialistic culture, the willingness to spend money in God's work or in his service is one of the greatest expressions of our commitment to live out the lordship of Christ.

b. *Subsidies.* Before we drain the church budget of more money, we might try to find other people who would subsidize student scholarships. The most effective subsidies are gifts from other students. Some young people have jobs that provide them with substantial extra money. If we challenge these students to assist those who have little or no money, the atmosphere of community can be enriched.

Accepting money from others has its pitfalls, however. First, the person who gives the money may have a hidden agenda for how the money should be used. Parents may give a gift with the hope of their child getting more attention from the youth leader. Others who subsidize may want some authority in making decisions about the youth group. Even students helping other students can be negative if those who give make the recipients feel guilty or indebted in some way to them.

A second potential pitfall is the effect the subsidy approach can have on the youth worker's reputation. If subsidies are sought too often, people may avoid the youth leader because they fear he or she only will want more money.

c. *Low-cost/no-cost activities.* Marilyn and Dennis Benson's book *Hard Times Catalog* (Group Books, 1982) contains hundreds of ideas for inexpensive youth activities. Realizing that "more people are discovering a lack of 'fat' in budgets and wallets" and noting the increased media conditioning of teenagers to "desire things of the affluent society just as these times are passing away forever," the Bensons offer constructive and creative ways for youth leaders to work toward "zero budgeting."

d. *"Youth funding."* In an article entitled "Financing the Youth Program" (*Working With Youth: A Handbook for the Eighties* [Victor Books, 1982]), Leland Hamby suggests that young people can be directly involved in the budget in a way he calls "youth funding." Through regular offerings taken at their activities and Sunday school classes, students can create their own reserves to be used as needed in the ministry. "The guiding principle behind youth funding," he writes, "is that 50 to 100 percent of all offerings collected in the youth division go into a special youth fund. The remaining percentage, if any, goes into the regular church budget."

"Youth Funding" can be an excellent tool for teaching young people the disciplines of consistent giving and the tithe. The only drawback is that if 100 percent of the money collected goes back into youth group expenses, students develop a "giving to ourselves" mentality and are isolated in their giving from the rest of the church body.

e. *Fund raisers.* Although fund raisers are usually devoted to needs and projects outside our youth groups, there are times when fund raisers can be used to benefit people within the group. A family in special need, a ministry in which some of the students are involved, or a mission project on which students from the group will serve all can be the legitimate recipients of money raised by the group. The leader must be cautious to monitor the use of this money, however, to make sure that fund raisers don't become an easy way for students to finance activities or things that they should pay for themselves.

f. *Other budgets.* In some church settings, there may be more than one budget out of which the youth ministry can function. Some churches have separate budgets for the Sunday school, for example. Rather than taking money for youth curriculum supplies out of the youth budget, perhaps the Sunday school budget can cover this need. Missions budgets may help in providing scholarships for service projects. Transportation budgets may be the source of money needed to rent vans or buses for activities and retreats.

4. *Does the budget represent actual needs?* Inexperience in planning a budget can lead us to two extremes. On the one hand, we might fail to anticipate all the expenses and find ourselves out of money five months into a twelve-month budget. To prevent this extreme, we need to ask these questions to evaluate thoroughness:

a. *Does the budget allow for price increases?* The cost of renting a film in April (when the budget is presented) may increase by ten percent or more by the next February when we actually rent it.

b. *Does the budget reflect the entire ministry, not just the portion in which we are involved?* We will be inclined to skew the budget in favor of the ministries in which we are most involved. But overlooking aspects of the ministry in which we are not primarily involved can cause financial and relational tensions.

On the other hand, inexperience makes us prey to "wish-list" budgeting, which lists nonessentials and hopes that the finance committee will approve them. Does the youth group *need* video games? Do the volunteer staff *need* to go to Honolulu for training?

The wish-list budget is destructive because it diminishes the credibility and integrity of the youth leader, and it operates as a poor excuse for responsible planning. Remembering that we are stewards for God's money can help prevent this second extreme.

Responsible budget planning asks this question: What does our youth ministry *need* this year to accomplish our God-given purposes? We must be careful neither to overlook aspects of the ministry that will need financial support nor to disguise our "wants" as needs.

A SPIRITUAL PERSPECTIVE ON BUDGETING

When we step into the world of budget planning, we may succumb to the temptation to leave behind a spiritual perspective in favor of administrative expertise. But both are needed, and neither should be sacrificed for the other. Three biblical themes will help direct us as we plan our youth ministry budgets.

Prayer. God owns everything. Budgets are merely human tools to help us channel and manage the resources he has entrusted to us. We use budgets to help us to be responsible stewards. Pray for wisdom in establishing the budget. Ask God for the ability to think ahead with vision and thoroughness about financial needs. Trust God to be the supplier of all that is needed.

When our budget meetings evolve into fights over minute details on the budget or when our youth group is depressed because the budget got trimmed, the problem is rooted in our attitude toward God. Our anger or frustration is at times an indication that we have forgotten *who* is in charge. Prayer about the budget will keep the Provider in the forefront of our perspective.

Integrity. In light of the dishonesty and greed often associated with organized religion, it's essential that we approach the handling of money with a healthy respect. Being "above reproach" is essential if we are to glorify God in our use of money.

Work for the Lord. It may sound trite, but keeping in mind that God has called us to our ministry can help us plan an effective budget. This is especially true if we find budgeting to be tiresome or tedious. If Jesus is our ultimate boss, if the youth ministry is where he has assigned us, and if a budget is necessary for our ministry, then we should try to establish that budget—both for the ministry and to please him. If reviewed correctly, careful planning of the youth group budget can be seen for what it truly is—an act of obedience to the Lord.

12.
REVIVING YOUTH SUNDAY SCHOOL AND BIBLE STUDY

My friend John heads up a dynamic youth ministry. His youth group has weekly outreach events, a great midweek meeting, and a solid program for training youth to grow as leaders. But his youth Sunday school is barely alive. Less than ten percent of the youth group "regulars" make the effort to come out on Sunday mornings.

John's problem seems to be typical. Few youth groups—whether active or not—make Sunday school a priority. Youth publications even reflect this situation: We can find resources on retreats, social activities, service projects, youth choirs, and fellowship—but very little about making Sunday school effective with teenagers.

For the teenagers of our particular congregation, however, Sunday school is the largest weekly youth activity. The majority of our junior high and senior high students come regularly to a Sunday school that provides our most effective platform for relationship building, outreach, leadership training, and Bible education. In fact, we actually have students come to retreats and activities because they were first recruited through Sunday school.

Because of our experience, I'm convinced that the youth Sunday school can be a living part of an effective youth ministry, helping students continue in Christian education and enabling them to see themselves as part of the whole church. As our ministry has developed, I've observed several characteristics that can contribute to the success of any church or youth group.

RELEVANT BIBLE STUDY

A recent survey of American teenagers revealed that ninety-five percent of those surveyed believe in God and that ninety percent pray. Yet only thirty-five percent could name five or more of the Ten Commandments, and only three percent could name all ten. Of those who attend church regularly, twenty percent don't know why Easter is celebrated, and fifty percent couldn't name the four Gospels.

Obviously our young people need to be taught the Bible. Fortunately the adolescent years are a time of inquiring, and teens want to know *why* we believe what we believe. So Bible study is a natural.

But Bible study of some random topic is hardly enough to hold our young peoples' interest. They must find the study relevant to daily living. In our Sunday school, we discuss how Christian faith relates to cheating, language at school, relationships to parents, the world of rock music, MTV, and promiscuous sex. Our students come because we try to give honest yet compassionate teaching about the challenges and costs of being a Christian in our world.

The effective youth teacher, then, must learn the teenager's world and must address the Bible's truth to that world. Tom and Betty, two of our former teachers, were good examples of this principle. They started their lessons with illustrations from the students' worlds and wove relevant applications throughout. To be effective this way, however, Tom and Betty had to work at it by listening to the radio, watching television, visiting campuses, and initiating spontaneous conversations with the teenagers.

The greatest problem in most youth Sunday schools is the tendency to move through a prepared curriculum with no attention given to the particular needs of the class members. In some classes, we've found it helpful to modify the curriculum so that the students can talk more. Sometimes the curriculum is temporarily discarded altogether in favor of a discussion about a class member's personal questions.

In every situation, effectiveness depends on meeting whatever needs are present. One young woman in our church, for example, comes to Sunday school because she wants to know the biblical responses to a cult group that is aggressively recruiting her. Another boy comes because his non-Christian parents are promoting a lifestyle that he finds unacceptable; he wants to find out what the Bible has to say about sex, family, and commitment. These students and others realize their need for answers to life from God's perspective, so relevant Bible study is vitally important to them. Nearly half of our young people come to Sunday school just for the Bible study because they want to know God's answers.

ACTIVITY AND VARIETY

Few adults can remember from their own youth the intensity of the average teenager's metabolism. Adolescent bodies and minds simply work faster than ours. The thought of a thirty-minute lecture might be tolerable to us, but to them it is torture.

In addition to being relevant, then, youth studies must be *active*. Active learning means discussions, interaction, and anything else that invites participation. For the junior high student, crossword puzzles and skits are more palatable than lectures. For the senior high student, active discussion and idea sharing helps develop reasoning abilities.

I think of Phil, who was shaky in his faith when he started in our Sunday school. Though he was introverted, he was an excellent actor. When he began taking part in Sunday school skits, he found an outlet through which he could grow. The active learning of role playing stimulated his mind.

Teenagers also become easily bored. Even the most relevant, active classes can become dull. The solution to this problem, then, is variety in teaching styles.

We've found that an educational film can be useful occasionally, and a guest teacher can offer some new insights. We sometimes add singing to the youth Sunday school, which adds a dimension of worship. The basic approaches that we alternate are occasional lectures, small groups, and question-and-answer times, which we call the "Open Forum."

CARING

The other half of our youth come to Sunday school consistently because they are cared for. A seminary assistant has worked hard to help us keep a ratio of one group leader for every eight students, and that makes it possible for lots of individualized attention.

Outside-of-class contact is the crucial ingredient in showing that we care. Through phone calls, birthday cards, visits to the schools, and social time together, our teachers build a rapport that facilitates learning.

The best example of this is Jerome. As a graduate student, Jerome has a full schedule, but he has made time for six guys who have never quite fit into Sunday school. He didn't start at church, however; he started on the basketball court. Jerome went out to dinner with his guys and let them know that he cared about them and their relationships to Jesus Christ. Those six guys have moved from total absenteeism in their sophomore year to near-perfect attendance in their senior year. The reason? They are eager to come to Sunday school to learn alongside Jerome, their teacher and friend.

Of course, we still have young people who are falling through the cracks. One young man came to me recently and said, "I've missed Sunday school for five weeks, and *no one* missed me." He was right, and we've had to make some corrections so that such an oversight wouldn't occur again.

SMALL GROUPS

Students grow most through personal interaction with both their teachers and their peers. For us, this realization has meant returning from a large-group format to small groups that are divided by grade and gender. The students complained at first because they had been accustomed to a big, rally-style Sunday school. But the smaller groups (eight to ten people per group) have increased our effectiveness in caring for students, in teaching, and in holding students accountable for their growth. The use of small groups also has increased our regular attendance by twenty-five percent.

Adolescent concerns differ greatly over the six years of junior high and senior high school. Junior high girls are wondering about makeup, dates, and getting married, while junior high boys might still be playing with GI Joe. Because of this wide diversity of needs, desires, and aspirations, keeping the groups small and divided according to gender helps the youth Sunday school meet each student as an individual.

WELCOMING OUTSIDERS

When a youth Sunday school group builds momentum, students and teachers build close relationships. Because of this warm fellowship, however, group members can become satisfied with the group as it is. The danger is that the group will fail to welcome new people because of the existing cliques.

Without the efforts of two students, Sharon and Holly, our group could easily fall prey to such exclusivism. Sharon and Holly recognized that it wasn't easy for a newcomer (or an "old-timer" who hadn't been around in a while) to feel welcome, so they formed a newcomer's committee. This committee welcomes people at the door of the Sunday school, registers their attendance, and escorts them to class. They also help the new person make several acquaintances, and they ensure that he or she is settled in a class.

Sharon and Holly recognized two things about new people: first, that they are scared to come into a new group, so they must be actively pursued and welcomed; and second, that being welcomed by a fellow student means more to a new person than a welcome by a teacher. Their perceptivity has made an important contribution to our program's success.

COMMITMENTS TO PRAYER

Times of discouragement are inevitable for those who work in youth Sunday school. Sometimes even after every student has been phoned personally, no one shows up for class. At other times, the lesson drags and the students seem asleep.

In these times, prayer—the active recognition of who is in charge of the situation—is the course to take out of the doldrums. Prayer is our access to God, who alone has the power to change the rebellious teen or win the professed agnostic. It's the support network through which teachers can be an encouragement to each other. The life-changing growth we desire to see through the youth

Sunday school occurs only when people and programs are supported through the ministry of prayer.

ADMINISTRATIVE ISSUES FOR THE SUNDAY SCHOOL

The qualities of caring and activity-oriented learning will help the Sunday school to improve, but administrative details can't be ignored.

1. *Attendance and registration.* How are we going to keep track of people? Will we use attendance cards? A computer list? Can we be both personal and efficient? Will students feel cared for if they get all their mailings by a computer list?

The best solution seems to be the assignment of one volunteer staff person to serve as class administrator. This person can

- welcome and register newcomers
- help group leaders follow up on absent students
- keep track of administrative details that can increase the caring function (birthdays, graduation, etc.)
- free teachers to build better one-on-one relationships.

2. *Room set-up.* More than a few youth leaders get distracted from the Sunday school program because of the responsibilities of setting up the room for the weekly program. When our goal is to relate to the young people, the folding and unfolding of chairs seems perfunctory. What can be done?

In some settings the answer is to get to the meeting room early. In my first year as a youth Sunday school teacher, I arrived an hour before class, set up every chair, and used the time to pray for the students who would sit in those chairs. Handling these administrative responsibilities didn't do much for my use of time, but it certainly helped me enter every class with an attitude of prayer.

Later I recruited others to help in the setup. Volunteers could help when we were the first group of the day to use the room, but now, with several groups using the same room during a Sunday morning, we have less than twenty minutes to rearrange the room for class. At present we have no master plan; we recruit anyone who is willing to help.

122

Room set up also raises other questions:

a. Do we want small or large groups?

b. If we want small groups, will we put the chairs in small circles (which promotes conversation and closeness) or will we put chairs around tables (which helps students write on worksheets or in notebooks)?

c. Will we have extra supplies on hand (Bibles, paper, pens)?

d. Will teachers need overhead projectors, blackboards, or video-playback machines? If so, where are the extra overhead pens? Who is in charge of getting this equipment? (Many churches don't have enough audio-visual equipment to go around, so it must be requested in advance.)

e. Will we provide refreshments? Who will get them, set them up, and clean up after the meeting?

f. Will we need a sound system?

g. Who is in charge of the cooling or heating system? (We have spent more than a few Sundays either freezing or sweltering because no one knew where the thermostat was.)

3. *Curriculum*. The use of Sunday school curricula adds a variety of other administrative requirements to the youth leader's "things-to-do" list:

a. When do we order the materials? Most curricula are for year-round use; will we use it year round? When do the teachers or small-group leaders need to begin their preparation with the curriculum?

b. Can we afford using a published curriculum? If not, can we order just the teacher's guides or the handouts?

c. Where will it be sorted? In my car? (Don't laugh; some youth leaders have been forced to transport their "offices" in their trunks.)

d. If we decide to write our own curriculum, who will type it and get it copied for Sunday school use?

CHOOSING A CURRICULUM

Every youth leader will need to decide how to effectively use the Sunday school time. This decision inevitably will include the question of whether or not to use a published curriculum.

Dr. Robert Pazmiño of Gordon-Conwell Theological Seminary proposes six questions that can be used to choose the best curriculum for our particular group:

1. *Theology*. Does the theology of the publisher and curriculum writers agree with the theology of the particular church or ministry? Are theological concepts presented which are appropriate for various age levels and comprehensive in exposure?

2. *Use of the Bible*. Does the curriculum affirm the Scriptures as authoritative and fully inspired? Is the whole counsel of the Scripture addressed in the sequence of the curriculum across the age groups?

3. *Educational methods*. Are the activities for learners varied and relevant to their life situations? Are students actively involved in the learning and challenged to deal with appropriate questions of the Christian faith?

4. *Teacher support*. Do the lesson plans allow for adapting materials to deal with time constraints, available resources, class size and differing student ability? Can inexperienced teachers effectively use the materials?

5. *Student interest and motivation*. Does the material deal with needs, interests, and concerns of the students? Are students provided with appropriate ways in which to apply biblical truth and encouraged to respond to the lordship of Christ in all areas of their lives?

6. *Design and appearance*. Do the layout, colors, and paper quality attract attention? Are racial and sexual representation appropriate? Can the curriculum be used more than once?

> The comparative importance of positive responses to each of these questions must be determined by those evaluating a variety of published curricula. Evaluators need to be aware of the strengths and weaknesses in any published materials and the unique needs of their particular educational setting. It may be helpful to develop scales for comparing curricula in the areas mentioned. Once a curriculum is chosen, the greater task is equipping teachers to effectively use and adapt that choice to their individual classes. Teacher training sessions can be planned to assist in this area.[1]

---

[1] Robert Pazmiño, "Facing the Difficult Task of Choosing a Curriculum," *New England Church Life* (Oct. 1984), 13.

13.
PLANNING YOUTH ACTIVITIES

What gives identity and cohesion to most youth groups is the weekly or monthly activities, which build group comradery and foster positive peer acceptance. Some groups have youth fellowships that meet on Sunday evenings; others have Saturday-morning breakfast clubs; still others have midweek meetings. For parachurch organizations and church groups alike, these meetings and activities build fellowship, foster outreach, and provide Christian, fun activities that give students alternatives to the drunken parties of some of their school friends.

WHAT DO WE DO?

Let's assume that our plans for Sunday school and the weekly Bible study are settled. Now we need to plan the extras—the programs that make our students proud to be part of our group or club, the programs that help us make a balanced effort to help meet the various needs in the spiritual, intellectual, social, and physical realm.

We need to plan gym nights, pool parties, trips to concerts, hayrides, "lock-ins," and progressive suppers. These programs may be the reason that students keep coming back for the Bible study. They may be the programs that will encourage group members to reach out to unchurched friends. These programs aren't simply peripheral aspects of the youth ministry; they are integrally important to a balanced ministry.

What is the best way to use our group time? Do we focus on

one kind of activity or do we try to do something different each week? Do we use prepared materials, or do we write our own?

If we choose to use published material the *Ideas* library (Published by Youth Specialties Inc., El Cajon, Calif.), *Group* publication and the *Any Old Time* series (Victor Books) are helpful either as supplements to programs or as the basic program model. If we choose to design a youth program and the regular group meetings ourselves, we have many options.

EIGHT STEPS FOR PLANNING ACTIVITIES

Although every program or meeting will have its own unique list of preparatory details, organizing youth activities involves eight basic factors.

1. *A plan.* First of all, we need an overall plan for the youth ministry year. If activities are to be useful and meet needs in our students, we must have some idea of where we are going. If we don't have a plan, our activities will be random and even purposeless.

Plans for the year should be related directly to goals. What is the overall youth ministry goal? If we can answer this, the activities begin to take on new meaning.

During our years of youth ministry, we have created several successful and not-so-successful activity plans. Two examples may help you plan your own activities.

PLAN A: From September through June, we held weekly programs that rotated activities in an attempt to meet special needs that couldn't be met in Sunday school, where the emphasis was on Bible study.

A week: Fellowship activity

B week: Outreach/service activity

C week: Fellowship activity

D week: Outreach/evangelistic activity

Comments on Plan A: Like all plans, it looked better on paper than it turned out to be in practice. Several months we had difficulty coming up with service projects (especially on our regular meeting night). We also had scheduling conflicts due to school schedules and holidays. Add to this the activities that didn't fit into one category (like retreats), and the weaknesses of the plan become evident. Nevertheless the plan did meet some significant student needs. The twice-per-month effort at fellowship was helpful in meeting social needs, especially because our students come from many communities and sometimes don't know each other. The alternating outreach effort helped add purpose to the fellowship nights (we taught students to serve each other so that we could serve those outside of our group), and the monthly evangelistic thrust helped us to keep from becoming ingrown.

PLAN B: From September through January, we focused on reaching unchurched students and training the Christian students in discipleship; from February through June, we focused on follow-up and student-led discipleship activities.

Under this plan, the fall and early winter were filled with evangelistic and pre-evangelistic activities (which give a visiting student positive feelings about the youth group and a brief, but general, introduction to the gospel). We also held special seminars for Christian students on "Being a Leader" and "Starting Your Own Bible Study." By February, we had many students to disciple, but the Christian students were too busy or too insecure to launch their own Bible studies.

Comments on Plan B: The plan looked good and gave us many ideas for the first half of the year, but programming for the second half of the year was difficult because of the students' broad range of needs. We had hoped that the Christian students would get busy with their own groups, but they never really owned the plan (see chapter 20).

In our situation, Plan A was relatively successful, but Plan B was poorly devised because it presumed five months of programming in response to the results of earlier activities. When the responses were not as we expected, our plans failed.

When constructing the overall activity plan, however, remember two things: first, remember the youth ministry's total program (if certain needs are being met elsewhere, don't focus on those needs in the weekly or monthly activity); second, plan for both churched and unchurched students (like Plan A above). It's easy to

127

focus either on one group or the other. If church students are obnoxious or rebellious, it's easier to think about the unreached (and ignore the church group). On the other hand, if we have a strong youth group with dynamic fellowship and growth, we may forget about those students who have no relationship to Jesus Christ.

2. *A purpose.* After we create a plan, we can design the individual activities. Each activity needs a purpose within the overall plan. Under Plan A, Christmas caroling at a nearby nursing home would have fulfilled our purpose "to reach out to those in need at least once per month" (week B). Perhaps it's artificial to separate the purpose of individual meetings from the overall plan, but it helps us design specific activities that are incomplete in themselves but that can contribute to the overall plan.

Several years ago, one of our basic purposes was to reach out to unchurched students who were on our Sunday school rosters but who never came. In response to this goal, one of our volunteer staff members started up a street-hockey program. Every other week, about a dozen guys would get together for a few street-hockey games that were held a few days before the regular weekly activities. Half of the students who came to the street-hockey games were in our target group. At first, they seldom came to anything but street hockey, but after eight months, several of them joined in on activities, and one of them came on a winter retreat—and became a Christian.

At first, the street hockey program seemed peripheral and unnecessary, but it served its purpose. It was one more way to incorporate new students into the group.

3. *Preparation.* After we've decided what activities fit into our overall purposes and plans, we need to prepare for the activity. At this stage the leader can assess what steps are needed to make the activity possible.

When I prepare an activity, I organize my thoughts on paper. At the top of the page, I list the primary and possible secondary goals of the activity. I then make a checklist of program responsibilities on the left side of the paper: promotion, place, personnel, order of events, etc. On the right side of the paper, I make a list of questions I have about the responsibilities. These questions help me see if there are any major obstacles that might keep us from having an activity.

Let's look at an example:

ACTIVITY: the annual mile-long sundae feed.

PURPOSE: Primary goal—to provide a fun, kick-off activity (in September) that will build youth group comradery and encourage students to bring their friends. Secondary goal—to help leadership team assess what kind of spiritual growth took place in those who went away to camp or on vacation with their families.

Ideas/details	Questions
Mile-long sundae	Where did we store the gutters?
Youth lounge	Is the room available? Do we have tarps to cover the new rug?
Speaker	Can we get a football player to speak on the kick-off theme?
Student testimonies	Who has had a meaningful summer?
Cleanup	What will we do with leftover food supplies?
Prizes for best eaters	Can we afford T-shirts as prizes?
Publicity	Can we have "Welcome back" postcards in the mail by September 1?
New youth staff	How can we introduce them to the students?
Personnel	Who can we recruit to do these jobs?

A list like this helps sort out jobs and responsibilities involved in planning the activity. Once we have determined the various responsibilities, we can decide who can best handle each responsibility.

4. *Promotion.* A responsibility that needs to be addressed early in the planning stages is informing students (and group leaders, if

they aren't involved in the planning) about the activity. Effective promotion informs students about the basic details of the activity (where, when, cost, etc.) and encourages them to come. For the church youth group, promotion can occur through a variety of channels:

a. *Promotion through the mail.* Mailing is effective:

- if the notices are creatively designed ("clip-art" books are creative tools).
- if the notices arrive *before* the activity (a problem with bulk mailings) but not so far before the activity that the students discard them and forget the announcement.
- if the notices are addressed to the student (addressing the notices to "the parents of. . ." may insure that students come, but it could offend the student).
- if the notices are sent to individuals (if three students live at the same address, send three mailers; one mailer will usually be read only by the one who gets the mail first).
- if the notices are sent regularly (if students aren't used to getting youth group announcements in the mail, they may not pay attention when the mailer comes).

b. *Promotion through the church or the youth group itself.* Bulletin boards, church calendars, and verbal announcements all can help to get the word out.

c. *Promotion through schools.* Some schools will allow posters to be hung or leaflets to be handed out. If so, this can effectively reach new students.

d. *Promotion through word of mouth.* This is the most effective means of communication, and it will provide the needed friendship gap left by posters or mailings. Students are far more likely to respond to a telephone call or personal invitation than they are to a poster.

5. *The place.* Educators are spending thousands of dollars each year to make classrooms more aesthetically effective in enhancing learning; from these experts, we can learn that the location of our meetings and the setup of our meeting place is important. When choosing a place for the activity, ask:

- What room is best for the group's size? The auditorium may be great for playing volleyball, but trying to get thirty-five students to sing in an auditorium built for four hundred may be frustrating. Consider what activities you will do throughout the meeting time. In certain cases, two rooms may be needed.

- Who will set up the room for the activity? Careful setup will save time at the start of meetings. Communicating exact instructions to the setup person(s) is essential.

- Do I have the keys to get into supply closets or rooms? If the custodian goes home at 5:00 P.M., the volleyball game might be cancelled if no one can get to the equipment needed for the evening meeting.

- Do I have at hand all the needed supplies or equipment? The momentum of the meeting can be destroyed if the leader needs to leave to get supplies.

- What environmental impact will the activity have on the meeting place? I remember one relay race that included bobbing in water for apples and using our teeth to find candy buried in flour (get the picture?). The water and flour mixed to make little biscuits that got ground into the rug and required special rug cleaner to remove. Perhaps we should have saved that relay race for the parking lot!

- What cleanup needs to be done? Activities with young people can yield mounds of trash—from tattered newspapers to scattered toilet paper to leftover food. Failure to plan adequate cleanup will result in one of two undesirable things: either it will be a late night for us as we clean up alone or we'll alienate the person or people who have to clean up after us.

6. *Personnel*. Who will help us during the activity? Preparation for activities includes the recruitment of people—both leaders to work alongside us and others who will serve behind the scenes. These people may include

a. *Sponsors or chaperones*. These volunteers may seem to be only along for the ride, but their purpose is to help maintain order, to reach out to the loner, and to provide adult supervision. Depending on the activity, the ratio of sponsor to student will vary. On an activity like an "all-nighter," we have one sponsor for every eight or nine students. On a group trip to a Christian concert, we may have one leader for every dozen to fifteen students.

b. *Co-leaders*. These can be students or volunteer staff who assist in the leadership of the activity. These could include the people who collect tickets, the person who runs the projector, or the person who will share his or her testimony. Planning the activity means that each involved person knows his or her assigned task and is thus prepared to act.

c. *Drivers*. For activities outside of a central location, drivers may be needed. These can be either students or adults; if students drive, however, make sure their parents know they will be driving. Make sure the drivers know the times of the activity, directions to the place of activity, whether or not they will be reimbursed for gas, and other responsibilities you need them to fulfill.

d. *Others*. People who will lead music, perform in skits, and provide refreshments are but a few of the potential others who may be involved in the leadership of an effective activity.

7. *The program*. One of the great paradoxes that I have observed in my years of youth ministry relates to youth activities: although teenagers love to be spontaneous and free flowing, they also like to participate in a well-administered program. They like spontaneity, but they also like a meeting with direction. Nothing turns them off faster than a youth leader who stands up front week after week and says, "Well gang, what shall we do this week?" They expect leadership and programs with purpose and direction.

In the administration of youth activities, the "program" is the "batting order." The program is the schedule of what happens next, who is speaking, who is praying, or who is leading the game. Students and staff alike benefit from a program.

A good program lists at least three basic facts:

- the order of events
- the people responsible for those events
- the approximate times assigned to these events.

Here's a sample program from one of our special outreach meetings:

6:30 P.M.	Leaders meet for prayer	Paul
7:00 P.M.	Brief team leaders	Tom
7:15 P.M.	Welcomers in place	Lisa
7:30 P.M.	Band plays ten minutes	David
7:40 P.M.	Introduction to evening	Tom
7:45 P.M.	Group competitions	Tom/Team leaders
8:15 P.M.	Introduction of Band	Paul
8:45 P.M.	Drama team performs	Jeff & students
8:55 P.M.	Summary message	Paul
9:10 P.M.	End	

To facilitate the smooth operation of such an activity, we made enough copies of the program for every participant. The times were flexible, but the evening moved right along because everyone knew what was happening next.

If more than a few people are to be involved, a written program is a necessity. Then, after checking over their respective parts, people can ask questions, revise what they might have planned, and fit together to make the activity a better success.

The use of an actual program is, of course, related to the nature of the activity. Going to the baseball game together needs only a few details: departure time, drivers (or bus captain), and expected return time. Other activities, like the thirty-hour "planned famine," make an official program mandatory so that all who lead can coordinate their efforts.

8. *The postlude.* All of us know the joy or relief of coming to the end of a particularly grueling activity. The task is accomplished, the students are sent home, and our work is done. Right?

Wrong. Effective youth ministry planning and administration requires follow-up to the activities we coordinate. It may not need to be done immediately, but we lose two growth opportunities if we overlook follow-up. First, good follow-up will enable us to grow through evaluation. As we ask ourselves how we did, we find out ways that we can improve programs and activities in the future. The comments of students as well as co-leaders should not be ignored. Instead, we should hear both the positive and negative evaluation so that our ministries can grow.

Follow-up to activities provides a second growth opportunity—affirmation. After an activity, I make a list of every student or adult who contributed to the activity. Then within a week, I try to send that person a note of appreciation for his or her participation. It could be as simple as "Thanks for having the courage to share your testimony," to "I appreciated the fact that you were a good sport when you got that pie in the face." This type of follow-up is our opportunity to say to others, "This ministry would not be the same without you; I appreciate you!"

Using this opportunity to affirm can cause great growth in us and in the people in our ministry. It can help us to be more grateful (something we all need in a ministry where it's easy to find things to complain about). It's also a powerful way to build students. When one student got my note thanking him for his help on an inner city work day, he told me that my note was the most important motivation for making him want to serve in the city on a week-long team the next summer.

In all of our preparation and planning for activities, we must keep our eyes on the ultimate goal—growth in the lives of the people in our ministry and of those being reached by our ministry. The reason why we endure practical jokes, water balloons, blundered activities, and long hours of preparation is to see our students grow in every dimension possible. The details of activities are important if we are to produce effective and cohesive youth programs, but the growth adds long-term meaning to all that we do.

14.
PLANNING FOR JUNIOR HIGH STUDENTS

The period of preadolescence or early adolescence demands special sensitivity in the youth ministry and program. Junior high students have specialized needs, and if we are going to reach these students effectively, we must organize our ministry to respond to these needs.

What is the junior high student like? Adolescents feel "unplaced" in society, according to Dr. David Elkind (*All Grown Up and No Place To Go*). They often feel they have no niche to fit into—a feeling psychologists call "anomic." Junior high students especially suffer from this insecurity. Unlike high school students, who know the lingo, music, dress, and values needed to survive in the youth culture, junior high students enter the adolescent world untrained and naïve. What is expected of me? How do I act? What should I wear? These and 1001 other insecure questions help make up the very special world we call junior high.

The special world of the junior high student requires a unique program. To blend the junior and senior high groups can harm the younger students. First, the junior high students' desire to achieve acceptance with their older peers may cause them to act or talk much older than they are. In this case, the junior high students are cheated from the freedom to grow up at a normal pace. Second (and this is the far more damaging result of blending the two groups), junior high students may find their fragile sense of self-worth easily damaged by older teens. The older students are usually more athletic, more coordinated, more popular, and taller.

In addition, the older students—who have learned to deal with their own insecurities by mocking others—will verbally abuse the junior high students in an effort to feel better about themselves. The result? The junior high students are reduced to being the "dogs" of the group.

In either case, the junior high students are hurt and may be lost to the group at a time when it's critical for them to find the love and acceptance they need. For these reasons, it is wise to separate the junior high program from the high school program. Occasionally the groups can be combined, but the growth and relationship-building times—Sunday school, the regular meeting, discipleship groups—should be kept separated.

Ministry to junior high students requires not only special programs but also special leaders.

CONSIDERATIONS FOR JUNIOR HIGH LEADERS

Dan Mahoney, who has led our junior high ministry for the past three years, has taught me much about what it means to minister with and to junior high students. He believes that junior high leadership requires special qualities and skills, and he looks to build these twelve factors in his own life and in the lives of people who work with him.

1. *Discipline.* Since junior high leaders are examples to the students, they must be self-disciplined before they can effectively disciple others. This discipline needs to be honest, letting the students know that the leaders still struggle. At a time when students are the most malleable, the leaders must set a good pace for growth.

2. *Vision.* The junior high leaders must be able to see the potential in their students. The idea that "we're just helping them through until they get to high school" is harmful; effective junior high leadership implies a vision that believes in God and in his desire to work through the junior high young person.

3. *Wisdom.* Junior high leaders need great wisdom in handling the students' multi-dimensional needs, the parents' concerns, and the church's expectations. Such wisdom includes knowing when to

discipline, how to address sensitive issues (like sex), and how to comfort frantic parents.

4. *Integrity.* Junior high students need leaders who are reliable and trustworthy. If a leader promises to call, that leader had better call! If a student is promised a visit, don't let him or her down. Integrity is essential in building trust in relationships with junior high students.

5. *Humor.* The ability to laugh, especially at oneself, is essential because it communicates to the junior high student a freedom to accept life. In many of the crises that junior high students experience, the issues are minor—at least from our adult perspective. If they can see us laugh at ourselves, they may begin to laugh at themselves in a healthy way, realizing that their "crises" are not so critical after all.

6. *Anger.* Building a junior high student's security in the youth group doesn't mean that the leader must be a punching bag or a doormat. There is time to rebuke irresponsible behavior with a healthy anger. During a recent obstacle course, Joe was acting up and stepped on the apparatus that another group was climbing on, causing fourteen other students to tumble. When the junior high leader saw this, he grabbed Joe by the collar, took him aside, and said, "Do that again and I'll tie your neck in a knot!" The anger let Joe know that his irresponsible behavior would not be tolerated. Moments later that same leader was cheering Joe on during another event.

7. *Patience.* Junior high leadership requires patience—patience to listen to the student who calls you on the phone to talk about "nothing special"; patience to deal with the silliness of junior high giggling; patience to live with the high energy level of seventh-grade boys. I remember one Saturday night when I was mingling with some of the junior high boys after the activity was over. We started wrestling, and it took only minutes for a mock "rumble" to ensue. When the parents arrived to pick up their children, they found me in the middle of the pile of twelve junior high students. I'm sure they wondered, "We sent you to seminary for this?" Junior high leadership means patience with the metabolic frenzy that accompanies the junior high years.

8. *Friendship*. The ability to be creative in building friendships with students is necessary for junior high leaders, because junior high students need friends. They need the unconditional love and acceptance of adult leaders because students usually will not get it from their peers (and frequently they are not getting it at home).

9. *Tact*. The story of the leader's rebuke to Joe shouldn't be taken out of context. This leader had a solid relationship with the boy, and he rebuked him in that context. Too often, junior high leaders see themselves as gestapo-like authorities who swing their "chains of command" in order to whip the junior high students into shape. Obviously this is to err on the side of harsh discipline. The junior high leader needs tact, the ability to decide when and how to discipline as well as the ability to affirm and encourage.

10. *Inspirational power*. Although I'm not in favor of the "you-can-if-you-think-you-can" philosophy that promotes human effort to an extreme, I do believe that junior high leaders function best when they can get genuinely excited about the potential of their students. If leaders can help the students accomplish some success, the students will feel more secure in their abilities and relationships. Ridge Burns and Linda Stafford emphasize this point in their book *How To Plan and Direct Junior High Super Stars:*

> Junior high students have a tendency to "reach for the stars." They want to be the most popular, best athlete, brightest student, biggest clown. But, of course, not all junior highs are the best or biggest or the brightest. In fact, many young teens are none of these. Yet they all need to see that they have "done something right." Thus, a junior high leader should provide opportunities which will allow all his junior highs to experience success.[1]

11. *Ability to listen*. Some junior high students are jabberers— all they do is talk, talk, talk, with little or no substance to the words. It's almost as if they are talking to fill the space while they think of something significant to say. Others are totally silent; to get them to say more than "yup" or "nope" is a miracle. So how do we listen? We need to listen to all facets of junior high students' communication. Body language—eye contact, posture, or stuttering—can tell us something about students. Language can tell us

---

[1] Ridge Burns and Linda Stafford, *How To Plan and Direct Junior High Super Stars,* (Wheaton, IL: Victor Books, 1983), 7.

what they may be hearing at home or from their peers. Their silence or boisterousness communicates to us whether they are listened to anywhere else.

Beyond this, I believe that effective listening to a junior high student also means listening to ourselves. As a junior high girl tells me about her boyfriend, I try to remember how intense the feelings were when I was a junior high student. If a guy in the group gets cut from a junior high sports team, I can identify with his failure and his sense of tragedy because I remember how I felt as a junior high student.

12. *Ability to affirm*. Writing notes of affirmation is a powerful ministry. A thank-you note or a simple "I was thinking about you today; I remembered to pray for your math test," can tell a junior high student that he or she is important or that you care. The note is an affirmation that keeps on affirming too because it can be read and re-read. I have found notes of encouragement in students' Bibles and schoolbooks, a testimony to the fact that students save these special sources of encouragement and refer to them occasionally.

CONSIDERATIONS FOR JUNIOR HIGH STUDENTS

When we start planning the junior high program, we start by looking for leaders who are sensitive (or who are willing to be trained) in a special way to young teens. But what about the junior high students themselves? What should we know about them as we plan their programs?

1. *Early adolescence is a traumatic time*. Starting about grade five or six, students anticipate adolescence. Their television shows build their expectations, and the advertising aimed at them causes them to desire this phase. For most students, however, the early period of adolescence is very awkward. They enter into the stages of adolescent growth ill-equipped and often uninformed about the challenges they will face. Thus, it is a traumatic time.

Physical growth results in a heightened self-consciousness that yields hours in front of the mirror worrying about head size, nose shape, breast development, or lack of muscle tone. Socially, they become aware of dynamics like peer pressure for the first time.

They are thrown into an insecure junior high culture where the first and most basic goal is survival, and this survival may require that others get put down or stepped on along the way.

The insecurity and trauma of the junior high years mean that our programs must be built toward the goals of building positive relationships among these students—both with themselves and with others. Ridge Burns writes, "I believe that we need to enable students to be sociologically comfortable before they'll become theologically aware. In other words, we need to build into our programs . . . events that will help kids know one another, learn to relate to one another, and affirm one another."[2]

2. *Junior high students' metabolism runs high.* This is a very basic observation for the person working with junior high students, but if we don't consider it in our programming plans, we could set ourselves up for failure. Having the refreshments just before the Bible study may be suicidal if the students get pumped up with sugar just before they are asked to sit and meditate on a passage. Reprimanding students for their restlessness during a fifty-minute lecture seems unreasonable; perhaps it is the speaker who should be reprimanded for not being sensitive to his or her listeners. Planning according to the metabolism of junior high students means that we think about at least three facets of every program:

a. *Timing.* The serious part of the meeting should come at a time when the students are a little tired (from some physical activity) but not exhausted (late on a Saturday night after a day of skiing, a big supper, and an evening full of skits).

b. *Activity.* We can't be impatient with students if they want to jump around a little (or a lot). Their bodies are going at a different speed than ours, and an effective program builds in activity to cater to their needs. Adults may enjoy sitting around the fire and talking with friends; but junior high students aren't quite so mellow.

c. *Endurance.* In spite of their hyperactivity, junior high students don't have much endurance. Our junior high group liked the idea of an "all-nighter" (probably because they had heard so much about it from their older siblings), but few of them made it through the night, and those that did got sick from over-tiredness.

[2] Ibid., 4.

Effective junior high programming must take into account that the junior high student's metabolism operates in spurts. Or their attention span may be very short. Or they may get tired even with fun activities if the activity is carried on too long.

3. *The junior high student's social experience is limited.* With the exception of those students who may have been previously involved in Scouting, Brigade or Pioneer Girls, or a local Boy's or Girl's Club, the junior high group may be the first non-school coed group that our students have ever experienced. We should keep this in mind as we plan youth activities because—

- students will not understand why it is important to come to the group unless we win them through relationships and a strong atmosphere of group acceptance; their concept of group identity is still being formed.

- students will lack a sense of propriety in their humor; they will not be able to discern between the appropriateness of the belching contest in the boys' cabin and belching in the back row during the evening church service.

- students will be awkward in boy/girl relationships, thinking that having a girlfriend or boyfriend is a requirement for coed group involvement. Thus, we must try to plan activities that encourage friendships that are not romantic.

4. *The junior high student's sense of sexuality is just forming.* The outcome of this in our programming may be seminars for young men and women on sex, sexuality, and relationships. It is far better that they learn these things in a Christian context than that they rely on peer rumors or even the amoral teaching of many sex-education programs. Although many parents teach about sexuality at home, most parents will welcome any help we offer.

This developing sense of sexuality has other implications for our programming. It will mean that we should work to provide good male and female models for our students without catering to the stereotypes of the media or culture. It also will mean that we should be sensitive to the coed games we plan. Games that emphasize height can demoralize junior high boys and embarrass the tall, junior high girls. Games that require lots of touching can

141

embarrass everybody—both the shy students who have never bumped into a member of the opposite sex and the curious student (who always wondered what it would be like to "goose" a girl).

5. *The average junior high student has poor self-esteem.* There are many causes for this feeling in junior high students; just the fact that they are "junior" high students implies that they are inferior to older teens. Their size, social status, personal awkwardness, and physical appearance all can contribute to their feeling of worth-lessness.

When we plan our programs for junior high students, we can help to address this problem in direct and implicit ways. Directly we can be excited about them, call them positive names (like "Super Stars," "Heroes," or "Dynamos"), and sponsor activities that guarantee their sense of success. Implicitly we can build toward better self-esteem in our students by discouraging the self-denigrating talk that often penetrates our students' conversations with each other. We also can avoid the activities or programs that create laughter at the expense of a student. (If we do practical jokes in our youth group, we can either let a staff person bear the brunt of the laughter, or we can warn the student participant in advance and applaud him or her afterwards.) We can also build toward positive self-esteem by making sure that rebukes or disciplinary actions take place as much as possible in a one-on-one context rather than in front of other students.

6. *The junior high ministry is a "hinge" time in the lives of our students.* It is during the early teen years that many students will decide whether or not they want to follow Jesus Christ, and this decision may be a direct result of the acceptance they feel in the junior high group or the degree to which they see the Bible applied to the problems that directly concern them.

The good memories and experiences of the junior high program will be the hinge on which future decisions will swing. Jamie, a high school junior, still feels alienated in our youth group. I was amazed at this because she has received lots of attention from fellow students and volunteer staff, but then I found out that her junior high leader had been very insensitive to her and had given her a bad junior high group experience. Now, three years later, she is still having a hard time trusting youth group members and leaders.

Jon and Glenn are more positive cases. Their positive relationships with their junior high leaders and with each other was a product of a very affirming junior high program. Jon and Glenn are now in college, but their junior high group experiences are wonderful memories that helped them make deep and positive commitments to Christ.

7. *Junior high students are not mobile.* This point may not seem to fit with the previous ones that dealt more with psychological or social dynamics, but it is important to consider in programming for junior high students. They simply have a more difficult time getting around. Unlike the high school group, where over half of the group members may have driver's licenses and access to cars, the junior high ministry is totally dependent on the assistance of leaders and parents. The frequency and location of programs, therefore, should take this reality into account so that parents are not made into taxi drivers and leaders are not exhausting themselves by driving around.

CONSIDERATIONS FOR PARENTS OF JUNIOR HIGH STUDENTS

The junior high years are traumatic not only for the junior high student but also for their parents. In the years of early adolescence, the parents are confronted with the reality that their "little boy" or "little girl" is indeed growing into adulthood. The start of questions about sex, the pursuit of certain friends (even if mom or dad doesn't approve), and the keeping of secrets by the junior high student can traumatize parents. If we are to be effective as leaders, we need to be sensitive to these parents as we plan our ministries. As we consider the junior high program, we can:

1. *Be sensitive to parents' needs.* One ministry offers a parent support group, which meets simultaneously with the junior high activities. This enables parents to talk together about mutual concerns, pray about problems, and counsel each other about possible solutions.

Another group offers parents a seminar about early adoles-

143

cence (similar to the James Dobson *Preparing for Adolescence* program) designed to help parents know what to expect in the early adolescent years. This is especially helpful for parents whose first child is entering adolescence, because it helps the parents to identify normal issues without blowing them out of proportion.

2. Be sensitive to parents' schedules. The fact that parents have to drive their junior high students everywhere (not only to youth group but also to school activities and sports and music activities), means that parents are overwhelmed with the new demands and conflicts caused by their child. Suddenly, the family has fewer dinners together, more conflicts about weekend nights, and increased scheduling difficulties.

We can help parents in two ways. First, early in the activity season we can mail parents a thorough schedule of junior high activities; this will help them anticipate and plan ahead for activities. Second, we can develop car pools or transportation networks for youth activities. If we can support families in this way, they will be more likely to give their full endorsement to the junior high program.

3. Be sensitive to parents' fears. Some parents have a look of uncertainty on their faces when they drop off their children for the retreat. The parents are afraid that—even in the youth group— their child may be corrupted or that we'll let the students get away with behaviors that would never be allowed at home.

There is no antidote to this, but we can deflect these fears by communicating with the junior high families. If we let them know the retreat schedule, explain the rationale for the activity, or inform them on how we will handle disciplinary problems, we can help them realize that we have given thought to the program. The parents may not agree with our approach, but if they get the facts from us, they are able to decide for themselves if they want their children to participate.

Two years ago, our junior high team designed a special curriculum for teaching junior high students a Christian view of sex and sexuality. To protect the parents from unnecessary fears about what would be covered, the junior high leader sent to the parents a letter that explained the content of the seminar. The letter openly invited parents to keep their teenager from the program if they disagreed with what would be covered. Parents went out of their way to express their appreciation for the letter because it removed their fears of the unknown.

CONSIDERATIONS FOR THE PROGRAM

Now that we have thought about all of the people affected by our junior high programs, we can start to construct a plan. When designing a junior high program, seven questions can give us perspective on what we will do.

1. *How often will we meet?* Will weekly meetings be too demanding for either parents or students? Should we meet during the week or on the weekend? What other church or community activities are putting demands on family schedules? We can design programs more effectively if we have adequate answers to these questions.

2. *How many leaders will we need?* With junior high students, we like to have one adult for every four students because junior high students need more supervision. Even though this creates more recruitment activity for us, having more adults involved may solve some car pool problems, and it certainly will help us reach the shy student or the outcast.

3. *How will we mix students?* In light of the heightened self-consciousness of junior high students, mixing students from different schools or having coed groups may be more difficult than we think. We need to think of programs or activities that will help students feel comfortable as they get to know each other.

4. *How can we plan for growth?* The shortened attention span combined with the low self-esteem means that our programs should include variety and activity without a lot of win/lose situations. If students come to the junior high group only to be on the losing team every week, they soon will withdraw from the group. Activity-oriented learning and fun games (which don't make fun of people or turn them into losers) can help us plan for effective youth group building with our junior high students.

5. *How can we draw them out?* Many junior high students are thinking about faith, their relationship with God, and the meaning

of their lives, yet few will articulate these thoughts. To find out what is on their minds, we must plan our programs to stimulate good questions. Role playing (with leaders doing the skit and students responding) as well as tough questions (like those raised in the two *Tension Getters* books) can be used to find out what students really think about Christianity and its relationship to real life.

6. *How can we affirm them?* Rather than designing a special program to help affirm her junior high girls, Cindy recruited them to work with her in her catering service. Through their success as caterers, the girls grew in their self-confidence. We need to plan for such affirming activities in our junior high programs. Service projects, visits to nursing homes, or fund raisers can help junior high students grow in their self-esteem as they are affirmed for their service to others.

7. *How shall we lead them?* Good junior high programming involves planning ahead about issues like discipline and rules. Although we can't possibly anticipate all behavior that will need discipline, we are wise to prepare ourselves by discussing hypothetical situations: what will we do if we find students making out under the pews? It's better to decide on an action ahead of time (call their parents and send them home) than it is to make up the rules after the incident. Making rules and disciplinary actions also enables us to communicate these facts to the students so that they understand their boundaries.

Wayne Rice of Youth Specialties has written the basic manual on junior high ministry (*Junior High Ministry, Revised Edition*, Zondervan, 1987), and he shares in it the realities of the joys and frustration of junior high work.

> Junior highers are stereotyped as being rowdy, restless, silly, impossible to handle, moody, vulgar, disrespectful, and worst of all, unpredictable. Unfortunately, all of these characteristics, may be true at times, but to be completely fair, the truth is that junior highers offer more than enough to offset whatever hazards may exist in working with them. They are, for example, tremendously enthusiastic, fun, loyal, energetic, open, and, most importantly, ready to learn just as much as the creative youth worker is willing to help them learn. The personal satisfaction and sense of accomplishment that are part of working with junior highers are unequaled anywhere else. (p 16)

Here is an exemplary vision of the potential in our junior high students, and if we keep this vision in mind as we plan our programs, we too shall achieve great satisfaction as we guide young people through a very traumatic period of their personal growth.

15.
PLANNING A RETREAT

I am convinced of the effectiveness of retreats. Over the course of my experience in youth ministry, I have seen more happen in the lives of students on retreats than almost anywhere else.

Retreats are excellent for building group identity, challenging students with the claims of Christ, and following up on discipleship relationships. Retreats give youth leaders a concentrated opportunity for leading students to a relationship with Christ, even as these students are able to experience his love through the relationships of the mini-community that can be formed on a retreat.

I am a believer in retreats for a personal reason as well: it was on a winter retreat in 1971 that I came into a personal relationship with Jesus Christ. My parents and a stubborn student recruiter finally convinced me to go—even though my life was in a state of active rebellion against God. I reasoned, "Well, the cute girls are enough to make up for the boring Bible studies." But God was at work on that retreat. Through the prayers of others and the working of the Holy Spirit in me, I came to a point of self-evaluation on the retreat. In the quietness of the New Hampshire woods, I came to see that God had a higher purpose for my life and that I could not outrun him. My life was changed on that retreat, and I have been privileged to see the same type of changes occur in many other lives since then.

WHAT IS A RETREAT?

Warren Bieble of the Singing Hills Christian Fellowship retreat center in New Hampshire has always contested the term "retreat" with me. He believes the better term would be "advance" because it is on these weekends that many students grow and go forward in their relationship with Christ.

Whatever the term we use, the idea is this:

1. The youth group goes away for the weekend (usually Friday night through late Sunday afternoon)

2. and has many opportunities for fun, outdoor activities (winter retreats may include opportunities for skiing, ski-dooing, etc.)

3. and for times of Christian teaching (either by a youth group leader or a guest speaker) that challenges students to evaluate their own relationship with Jesus Christ.

PLANNING THE RETREAT*

Every retreat and youth group is unique. The plans that have worked for last year's fall retreat will not work for this year's spring retreat. Every group and every retreat must be handled differently. However, we can make basic plans by asking ourselves several key questions:

1. *What is our goal?* Who are we trying to address with Christian truth? How will we do this? What types of fun will our youth group enjoy? These and a dozen other questions will help us clarify our goals.

The goal of the retreat must fit in with the overall plan for the youth ministry. As the yearly schedule is produced, we must see retreats as fitting into the other activities and programs. For example, our youth group holds three retreats each year: the fall retreat is designed to help welcome newcomers; the winter retreat is an evangelistic tool that helps our students' invited friends hear the gospel; the spring retreat is specialized training for those going out on summer mission teams.

Set realistic goals for the retreat. Don't expect a retreat to be the miraculous cure for problems within your group. In some

---

*See also "The Complete Retreat Outline," *Group* (May, 1983) which offers a helpful checklist for retreat planning. Write the publishers of *Group* magazine (P.O. Box 481, Loveland, Colorado 80539) for other helps for planning a retreat.

respects, a positive retreat is a result of, not the cause of, ongoing youth group health.

One youth leader was having a horrible year. Student morale was low, and parents were being negative toward him. He decided to plan a retreat to cure his ills. The retreat occurred, but rather than being the panacea that he had hoped for, it aggravated the problems. Students grew more discontented, and parents rose up with a fervor that eventually drove the man away from that church.

What happened? The intensity of the retreat brought all the group's problems bubbling to the surface. Perhaps they could have delayed the retreat until later in the year, or maybe he could have held a leadership retreat with those students whose attitudes were positive. He failed, however, because his expectations were too great for the retreat; his goals were not realistic.

Youth retreats *can* accomplish several goals:

a. Reaching out to the "fringe" students

b. Evangelizing the unchurched (and the Christianized rebels, as in my own case)

c. Building youth group identity

d. Training for Christian ministry (this is the goal of our Spring training retreat for summer mission teams; it was also the goal of a retreat in 1982, when students were preparing to be counselors at a Boston-area Billy Graham Crusade)

e. Rest and relaxation (although hard to imagine on many youth retreats, the serene atmosphere of many retreat centers allows our overly anxious, hurried teenagers to rest and relax from a hectic lifestyle)

f. Making positive Christian memories (retreats are among the most memorable experiences in many people's teen years)

g. Counseling the student from a troubled home (the concentrated time together allows students to open up more and to be available for counsel)

h. Modeling the Christian life (since staff and students actually live together for two and a half days, staff can demonstrate Christian behaviors like what it means to pray, how to study the Bible, and how to keep one's anger under control)

i. Preparing leaders (in addition to the three youth retreats, we have two staff retreats per year for the purposes of building our staff together for effective youth ministry)

2. *When shall we go?* There is no ideal time, although the fall and the middle of the winter are among the most popular times. The fall back-to-school retreat provides a great kickoff for group building as the year starts; the mid-winter retreat helps reshape group goals and provides a relief from the the middle of the winter blues (especially in areas with harsh winters).

When planning the time of the youth retreat, consider these factors:

a. *Youth group schedule.* Again, the overall plan plays a part in determining the best time for a retreat. Make sure the retreat is timed appropriately with other activities: don't schedule a retreat at the end of a busy month if the next month is without activities.

b. *Church calendar.* Some churches have family camps or other retreats that may compete for the teenager's attention. Spacing the dates of the youth retreat away from other church functions can help increase attendance.

c. *Holidays.* Although school vacation weeks and holiday weekends seem to be ideal times for retreats (especially for retreats of four to five days), they are also the times when families plan activities. Therefore a youth retreat during vacation times can put our students and their families in the difficult position of deciding between the youth group and the family.

d. *School year.* Will the fall retreat conflict with the opening day of football? Will the mid-winter retreat be held on the Saturday when many students will need to take the Scholastic Aptitude Test? Will the spring retreat overlap prom weekend? We must plan with school schedules in mind so that we can be sensitive to as many students as possible. However, we'll never find the perfect weekend. Occasionally we will have to make decisions that conflict with one or more of the students' other activities.

e. *Family finances.* Based on my youth group experience, I would love to have a retreat every month and forget the rest of the program. The biggest reason why this isn't possible is finances. Most weekend retreats cost between forty dollars and sixty dollars per person (even more if the costs of transportation or ski packages are factored in). If families have two or three children in the youth group, we are adding a great burden to their budget by having a retreat, especially if we plan the retreat at a time when their budgets face other demands, like Christmas. Financial aid and other creative budgeting can help us resolve the problems, but we must be sensitive to families before we plan retreats that are too frequent or too expensive.

3. *Where shall we go?* The location obviously depends on the size of the group, the time we are willing to travel to get there, the accommodations available, and what we can afford. We will want to consider several other factors.

Consider the youth group or church history. If the group *always* goes to a certain place, then perhaps we don't have a decision to make. On the other hand, we may be tired of the same old place and may need to explore a new facility.

Also consider the comfort factor. We have found that taking groups to YMCA camps with pit toilets and water from the nearby stream works if we tell students in advance about the facilities. Although camping is an inexpensive form of lodging, it can be a nightmare if the weather is bad. Most teenagers prefer surroundings that are a little more comfortable.

Consider your group's experience and expectations. An urban youth minister took his group into the Maine woods only to discover that it was too quiet for the students; several of them became nervous from the lack of noise!

Consider the organization of the facility. Will people be there to repair things? Will they take an injured person to the hospital? Do we have to do our own cooking? And will they allow us to plan our own program? This last question is important because the achievement of personal group goals is more difficult at a retreat center where we are forced to conform to someone else's program and schedule.

4. *Who will attend?* What age group of students are we targeting to reach? Junior high? Senior high? Collegians? The answer to this question helps us determine the program, the need for a speaker, and the number of staff people.

If we invite a guest speaker, we must find someone who is well equipped to address the age group on the retreat. Finding qualified people whose schedule is free on our weekend may be difficult; early planning (six to twelve months in advance) will give us more options. If we decide to speak ourselves, we can address the specific needs of our youth group, but we must be willing to delegate other leadership responsibilities so that we don't burn out on the retreat.

The staff/student ratio may need to be higher for a junior high retreat than for a senior high one. In recruiting leaders for the retreat, plan early; volunteers will need advanced notice to clear their schedules for a weekend retreat.

Will we need other specialized leaders? We occasionally have brought special leaders to lead the music for a weekend. Or we may want to invite a group instructor for events like skiing or hiking.

5. *How will we attract students to attend?* Creative flyers, retreat brochures, and handouts are all good recruiting or advertising tools. Church bulletins and mailers can remind families, and posters can remind students to plan ahead.

But the best way to get students to attend retreats is personal contact. Phone calls or personal invitations can really encourage students to come. Personal recruiting like this should be delegated to staff members and responsible students so that newcomers will be adequately cared for on the retreat. If I invite fifteen new students to the retreat and they all come, they will expect me to make them feel welcome and comfortable. It is unlikely that I can do this, so some students will have a bad retreat experience. It's far better for me to get fourteen others to help me invite people. This way the new people who come have one guaranteed friend who can be their personal host on the weekend.

As you plan recruitment, be aware that some students and parents are notoriously bad planners: they register at the last minute, sometimes even as the bus is preparing to leave. This makes coordinating the logistics for the retreat very difficult. Offering financial discounts for early registration or penalties for late registration and setting an attendance limit may help avoid last-minute registrations. We have considered rejecting last-minute registrants, but it sometimes has put us in the position of rejecting the students who most need to go on the retreat.

6. *How will we pay for it all?* Assuming that the retreat will pay for itself, what are the costs? In calculating the per-person costs, consider the cost of

  a. renting the facility

  b. food (and its preparation)

  c. transportation (see the options under question 7)

  d. the speaker (travel, food, lodging, and honorarium)

  e. staff (if they are giving up a weekend to minister, we like to cover their cost; if we do this, the student fee must absorb it)

  f. promotional brochures, mailings, etc.

  g. retreat entertainment (supplies for skits, rentals for movies, etc.)

  h. scholarships (if we want to sponsor students who can't afford to go, then we must build our reserves)

  i. insurance (if the church has to take out special insurance riders to cover the group)

Obviously if all these items are factored into the retreat cost, students would never be able to afford the retreat. The costs of *a, b,* and *c* alone make the retreat expensive enough. The best alternative is to factor some of the retreat budget into the regular budget (see chapter 11).

In our youth ministry, *c, f, g, h,* and *i* are all taken from other accounts. Other groups ask staff to pay part of the retreat costs (usually *a* and *b*). Some groups receive donations that are used for scholarships. Saving money on the speaker (using a local person rather than flying someone in), taking a school bus rather than a coach, and using the mimeograph machine for brochures rather than offset printing all can help lower the budget.

7. *How will we get there?* I once heard of a singles' ministry that chartered a jet for their winter retreat to Switzerland. Such transportation isn't available for the average youth ministry. Most of us choose between buses or cars. Some churches own vans or buses that can be used if qualified drivers are available.

Buses are advantageous because they consolidate the group, free the leaders to relate to students, and get the group to the retreat location at one time. Coaches have storage room, which helps transport cumbersome sleeping bags, skis, and other equipment.

However, bus rental is expensive, even buses whose rates are determined on a sliding scale. A school bus is cheaper than a coach; a bus without a restroom is cheaper than a bus with one.

Using cars is still the best option for the smaller youth group, and it may be an economic necessity for other groups. If we use cars, however, new questions arise:

a. Will drivers pay for the gas or will the youth budget reimburse them?

b. Do we have enough drivers to get both students and equipment transported? (The equipment can be shipped in a rented truck, which is still cheaper than renting a bus.)

c. Will students be allowed to drive?

d. How will we make sure that staff or student drivers have appropriate insurance and safe cars?

e. Will the drivers go up together or will they arrive at a pre-established time?

8. *How will we design the program?* The good news of a retreat is that we have consolidated time with our youth group, but the bad news is that this time can slip right through our fingers if we don't plan it well. The proper balance of fun versus challenge, relationships versus time alone, and free time versus structured time is all part of the management of the program.

Planning the retreat program leads us to further questions:

a. Who will be the emcee?

b. When will the speaker speak? (For how long?)

c. Where will we fit in singing, skits, ice breakers, or organized games?

d. When will we allow for daily devotions/quiet times?

e. Will students be required to attend every meeting?

f. When will the meals fit best?

g. When will we have outdoor activities, both organized and spontaneous?

h. When and how will we communicate the rules for the weekend?

i. Will there be a worship service? If so, who will lead it? When?

j. When is the best time to invite students to respond to what they have heard?

k. Will there be time for "How-God-spoke-to-me-this-weekend" testimonies?

l. When will we leave the retreat facility?

One of the basic ways we answer these questions in our youth group is through the production of two printed handouts. The first, a detailed schedule of the weekend, goes to our leaders—both student leaders and volunteer staff. This schedule should include the times for meetings, quiet times, singing, meals, free time, and lights out. It also details who is in charge of what responsibilities, and it offers comments or advice to the leaders such as, "During the quiet time hours, be looking for students who are alone and don't seem to know what to do; try to help them get started." (A sample handout is included at the end of this chapter.)

A second handout is a youth group notebook for the retreat. Use four sheets, folded in half and stapled, yielding an eight-page notebook that measures 5½" x 8". Use one page for the cover, one page for the basic schedule (which includes a written list of retreat rules), four pages for note taking on the basic sessions, and two pages of fill-in-the-blank Bible studies for use in morning quiet-time slots.

The communication of this basic schedule to staff and students helps offer a concrete outline for the weekend while leaving room for spontaneity. In general, it helps everyone feel more comfortable about the retreat program and schedule.

9. *Will we be prepared for contingencies?* We need to think about what we will do if certain problems arise. We have had a few major and minor flare-ups over the years, and although these incidents may seem catastrophic, they aren't. They merely are realities that must be dealt with—either by careful planning beforehand or by spontaneous responses on the scene.

a. *Weather problems.* Everyone is delayed five hours because of a snowstorm on the way up to the retreat; the group arrives at 2:30 in the morning. Or the Saturday afternoon free time is hampered by constant rain; all of a sudden, the lodge that was "so cozy" becomes claustrophobic because no one can go out.

Solutions: plan spontaneity into your schedules; remember to come up with some indoor activities in case of rain; be flexible (our godly response to these crises may be the best teaching tool we have).

b. *Transportation problems.* The buses don't arrive to pick up our group. Or the staff members' cars all freeze up because the temperature dipped to below zero.

Solutions: have the bus company's phone number with you; instruct staff to winterize their cars as needed; make sure someone has a credit card or some extra cash in case of emergency repairs.

c. *Someone gets hurt.* Dave stubs his toe and breaks it. Wanda finds out that standing on the toboggan isn't a good idea. Fred falls out of bed, or Cheryl hits her head on the ice. Each needs a trip to the doctor to get X rays or stitches or medication.

Solutions: have students' home phone numbers with you so that you can call parents for permission (we have stopped using permission forms because lawyers have told us that they can't stand up in court); have the church insurance numbers available; find out where the nearest emergency room is; have a first-aid kit with you; be sure to have a staff person with a car to drive the student to the hospital.

d. *Logistical problems.* The heat will not come on (or shut off). There aren't enough beds. The toilet gets jammed in the middle of the night and overflows into the hallway.

Solutions: at the beginning of the retreat, locate the person in charge of the camp; if possible, make a trip to the retreat location before the weekend so that the facility can be checked out.

10. *What about follow-up?* The retreat doesn't end when everyone returns home. The speaker, retreat center, bus company or drivers, and other specialized leaders have to be paid. Lost items need to be collected and either disposed of or stored at the church until someone claims them. Families of accident victims may need to be contacted so that parents get the right information from us.

Beyond the administrative follow-up is the spiritual follow-up. We may need to call the student who had deep personal questions about faith. New Christians must be invited to Bible studies or youth group activities. Counseling relationships that were formed need to be pursued so that students and families can be helped. Students who came for the first time to the retreat may benefit by receiving notes or follow-up phone calls.

OTHER "RETREAT-TYPE" ALTERNATIVES

The costs of retreats plus the busy-ness of some students may force us to come up with creative retreat alternatives that can stimulate the retreat experience without the cost of time and money that usually accompanies a retreat. The dynamics of the shared experience of a retreat can be duplicated, at least in part, by programs like

- Lock-ins or all-night events
- Day trips like mountain climbs or bike trips
- Mini-retreats at someone's home, Friday through Saturday or Saturday through Sunday
- Fund-raising projects like World Vision's "Planned Famine" or World Concern's "Refugee Camp."*

RETREATS: THE HOLY SPIRIT AT WORK

In a world that tends to separate us, the retreat experience is a rich opportunity to build a sense of Christian community in our youth groups. In the midst of the hectic schedules of our lives, we can say to our young people the same words that Jesus said to his twelve: "Come away by yourselves and rest awhile."

In the midst of that rest (which in teenage terms may mean fun, games, athletics, etc.), the Holy Spirit will work, and we can see lives changed. As we provide students with the opportunities to contemplate their personal commitment to Jesus Christ, they will respond by the power of the Holy Spirit at work. I believe it because a youth retreat changed my life, and I believe it because a youth retreat also changed Linda's life and Dave's life and Ray's life and Doug's life and . . . .

---

*World Concern offers a program that simulates 24 hours of life together at a refugee camp. Write for information to World Concern, P.O. Box 33000, Seattle, Washington 98133.

SAMPLE RETREAT SCHEDULE FOR LEADERS

TO: Youth Staff and Student Leaders
FROM: Paul Borthwick
DATE: January 20
RE: Winter Retreat—January 31–February 2

SCHEDULE AND DETAILS:

Friday (1/31)

5:30 P.M.	Registration period (1)
6:00 P.M.	Bus departs
8:30 P.M.	Bus arrives at Brookwoods (approx.)
10:30 P.M.	Singing and ice breakers (2), welcome, rules
	Talk #1: "How Can I Make Tough Choices?"
12:00 midnight	To rooms
12:30 A.M.	Lights out (or at least an attempt at it)

Saturday (2/1)

7:00 A.M.	Rise and shine
8:00 A.M.	Breakfast (3)
8:45 A.M.	Quiet times (4)
9:45 A.M.	Large group—singing, mixers, announcements (5)
10:15 A.M.	Talk #2: "Where Is God When It Hurts?"
11:00 A.M.	Small groups for discussion (6)
12:00 noon	Lunch
12:30 P.M.	Announcements about free time
	Brief staff meeting after lunch in dining area
	Free time until 5:30 P.M.
	Organized Games? (7)
5:30 P.M.	Dinner
7:00 P.M.	Talk #3: "What Does It Mean to Follow Christ?"
8:00 P.M.	Response time, small group discussion
8:30 P.M.	Fun time—singing, skits (planned and
	spontaneous), games, movie
12:00 midnight	Lights out

Sunday (2/2)

7:00 A.M.	Rise and shine
8:00 A.M.	Breakfast
8:45 A.M.	Quiet times
9:45 A.M.	Talk #4: "How Do I Deal with Loneliness?"
	Singing and worship to follow
	Sharing time
11:15 A.M.	Free time (8)
12:00 noon	Lunch
1:00 P.M.	Start to clean up
2:00 P.M.	Bus arrives, pack, depart
4:30 P.M.	Arrive home at GC

NOTES:

1. Tom and Tim are in charge of the registration period; when you arrive, please ask how you can help by either packing the bus or helping with registrations.
2. Kristy, please take charge of singing. Tom, please arrange a couple of ice breakers.
3. Encourage students to eat breakfast to maintain health.
4. Quiet time instructions are in the retreat notebook; please have a quiet time with a student if they look as if they are lost.
5. Tom is emcee; plan on 2–3 songs (perhaps a theme song?), 1–2 mixers
6. You'll form groups similar to your Sunday school small groups, and I'll offer some discussion questions for your groups.
7. This is an option, especially needed if there is bad weather.
8. This time on Sunday can be used for following through with students whose relationship with God you still question.

OTHER THINGS:

1. Kristy, please make sure we have songbooks.
2. Anyone who plays guitar is welcome to accompany Kristy; tell her of your interest.
3. Please be praying *every day* for God's Spirit to be mightily at work!

16.
SPECIAL MINISTRIES: CHOIR, DRAMA, AND MORE

Youth Sunday school, regular activities, and retreats all provide the basic foundations for an effective youth program, but specialized ministries within the youth program provide great opportunities for extra body building. It is through these programs that students learn to serve and to minister with others.

Each youth group and youth leader will have to decide which of the specialized ministries are best matched to a specific group situation. At Coral Ridge Presbyterian Church, where *Evangelism Explosion* was developed, the *Youth Evangelism Explosion* has become a dynamic feature of the youth ministry. At Wheaton Bible Church, the youth group has developed a Sidewalk Sunday School program that reaches out to latchkey kids in a nearby housing development.

Some groups pursue puppetry ministry, while others develop musical ministries like youth choirs, handbell choirs, or rock bands. Youth groups may choose to specialize in refugee ministry, urban outreaches, clown ministry, or drama teams—all depending on their situation, group size, and leadership.

Specialized ministries offer a youth group an increased sense of identity, opportunities for service, and a positive outlet for their active energies. But specialized ministries must be seen as *part* of the total ministry. Our youth mission teams at Grace Chapel, for instance, are part of the whole discipleship and leadership training emphasis in the group.

Specialized ministries are time consuming too. As youth

leaders, we can want to do everything with our groups. We read about one youth group that has twenty-five students on evangelistic teams, and we hear of another group that travels throughout the country with their drama team. We learn of another group that ministers in nursing homes through a youth choir and another group who evangelizes young children through a puppetry ministry. We learn about these specialized ministries, and we return to our youth groups hoping to start specialized ministries in evangelism, drama, choir, and puppetry. We forget that most youth groups can only do *one* specialized ministry well. The group with the powerful drama ministry probably doesn't have a great youth choir. Specialized ministry takes too much time and effort to do it all well. We have to choose.

Whatever our choice of specialized ministry, certain basic planning principles can help us develop a unique and effective ministry with our students.

GETTING STARTED

1. *Test the interest level.* Through either word of mouth or by a brief survey, we can find out what students are interested in doing. It would be hard to start a choir if less than ten students were interested, but a puppet ministry could conceivably be started with one or two students.

Testing the interest level also means some discreet testing of other factors like ability and experience. If three students have experience in playing piano, a youth choir becomes more feasible; students with drama experience or previous evangelistic training can contribute greatly to specialized ministries. However, a handbell choir with no experienced "ringers" will require more training and perseverance.

Find out if the interested students are available. The students with musical ability already may be committed to playing in the marching band, orchestra, and concert band. They may be capable but not available. Ability and availability must be balanced in the preparatory stages of special ministries.

Jeff Collins, who used to lead our youth choir and drama team, put it this way: "For a specialized ministry to work, students must *want it,* and they must have the *potential to do it.*" If the desire and some basic ability are present, then we can proceed.

2. *Talk one-on-one with interested students.* Individual interviews will help us uncover hidden talents as well as discover which students have the capability of leading their peers. In youth ministry, the leaders may not need to be the most talented students; they simply need to be the most motivated. Brett was our key student in Youth Evangelism Explosion because he was fired up about the program. He wasn't the best memorizer nor necessarily the best evangelist, but through his zeal, he was able to recruit a dozen other students.

3. *Don't be afraid to start small.* Too many times we are afraid that a small group will result in small results. This isn't the case, especially when it comes to building youth group momentum. If we can concentrate our efforts on the few students who are committed and interested, they in turn can influence their peers.

Several years ago, Mary Ann taught a Sunday school class on outreach to the urban areas of Boston. After her sessions with that class, two students were genuinely interested. Mary Ann poured herself into them, communicating her own commitment to the city to them. Through these two students, the whole youth group has been affected because these two challenged others to join with them. We are presently planning a specialized ministry called "Youth Bridge Builders," a youth ministry outreach designed to build bridges to churches and ministries in the city of Boston. All of this because two students got excited.

4. *Start with a success.* If only ten students indicate an interest in the youth choir, don't hold the first rehearsal in the nearest auditorium. Instead, hold the rehearsal in a small, empty room where the sound bounces everywhere, creating a sensation of great noise. The students who are wondering whether or not to join the choir will say, "Wow! We sound better than I thought!" And they will be excited to return to sing again.

In one of our greater mishaps in youth ministry, we had finally prepared the youth group to sing in the morning service. This was the first of what we hoped would be many such ministry opportunities, but the choice of songs was wrong. One piece, a dirge-like number by Handel, made the students ashamed to be singing, and we lost almost all our youth choir momentum. It would have been far better to start with a simpler piece.

5. *Recruit others as leaders.* An enthusiastic leader may be able to get students to join the drama team, but if that leader doesn't know the first thing about drama, students will quickly lose interest. The same is true of musical groups, evangelistic teams, and other specialized ministries. We need leaders with the ability and desire to lead.

When our drama team first got started, students were excited about the idea, but the volunteer leader had no real experience in drama. The drama team floundered until God gave us Pam, whose undergraduate studies, sense of call to ministry, and youth ministry experience all included drama. Through her leadership, the youth drama team became a solid *ministry*.

6. *Recruit key students.* Students, especially those who are recruited through a sense of call from God rather than a desperate plea from us, are the best builders of specialized ministries. When students sense that their ministry is their niche in the kingdom of God, they will grow dramatically and will recruit others to join them.

From a negative perspective, this is why our puppet ministry never got off the ground. One high school student had a vision for it, but he became possessive of it and criticized those who made attempts at it. The ministry soon lost its energy. Why? Because we had failed to train the student in his ability to understand a team ministry and because he "owned" the ministry to the point that others weren't allowed to join in.

7. *Advertise!* Get the word out. If our students are going to do specialized ministries, they must know about the opportunities that are there. Reminding students of rehearsals or meeting times is a necessary discipline. At the start of a ministry, postcards, phone calls, and even a personal shuttle service may be needed to get students involved.

A short notice in the church bulletin (or even the youth calendar) isn't enough. Few teenagers will respond to a tiny line that says, "Interested in the youth choir? Come to our first meeting Sunday afternoon at 5:00."

When a new ministry is starting up, special time must be given to it in youth group meetings and extra space must be given to it in youth group publicity. After it gets established, the publicity can diminish a little, but the initial stages require extra efforts.

BUILDING THE MINISTRY

When a youth choir, drama team, or puppet ministry is started, the potential for extra ministry (and extra growth in the lives of students who are involved) is exciting. Suddenly students can start serving others and, in the process, get their eyes off themselves. All of this growth, however, doesn't occur by accident. Leaders must work hard to keep the ministry growing in the right direction.

1. *Be flexible.* As students grow and their spiritual gifts start to become apparent, perhaps the group will change. Our youth choir of several years ago evolved into a drama team because the students demonstrated much greater success at communicating through acting than they did through music.

One group had an opportunity to minister to children. The group had prepared a number of dramatic skits, but they found that the skits weren't communicating. They rewrote the scripts and used puppets instead of actors. The children were much more responsive.

2. *Build students' commitment to ministry.* One of the sad aspects of some types of specialized ministry is that it can become "just a performance." The testimonies can be given without feeling, the songs sung without heart, and the plays acted out without any spiritual concern for the audience. The special ministry leader holds the key to keeping the ministry group on target through his or her teaching on what it means to do ministry.

Through our own examples, leaders can demonstrate that ministry is commitment more than it is feeling. We can show that we must pray and prepare, but the spiritual results belong to God. We can be the ones who honestly relate that our emotions don't always keep pace with the ministry, but that we can grow to serve others by depending on the Holy Spirit, even when we don't feel like serving.

3. *Keep a spiritual focus.* We also must help our specialized ministry teams keep a spiritual value system about their work. The ultimate goal is to glorify God though our service. We should remind our teams of this frequently so that other goals—like work accomplished, flawless performance, etc.—don't distract us from our ultimate purpose.

4. *Build a supportive fellowship.* We in Western society are much more task oriented than we are people oriented. As one person has put it, we tend to use people and enjoy things rather than enjoying people and using things. This task orientation can become dangerous on a special ministry team if we forget the importance of the fellowship within the team. A supportive fellowship can be the greatest source of growth, especially when the ministry team feels like a failure or feels as if God isn't using them. The support within the team—of prayer, mutual edification, and sense of corporate obedience to Christ—can make all of the hard work much more worthwhile.

5. *Highlight the team.* Having students report on what they are doing and how God is directing them can do two things. First, it can be one way of affirming the team and building their sense of confidence; second, it can be a great recruiting tool. Students who testify of how God used them through the youth choir or the drama team will challenge other students to be a part.

KEEPING IT GOING

As a specialized ministry grows, the leaders will face certain new questions, like:

1. Do we delegate the ministry to someone else?

2. Will this choir, drama team, or puppet team grow so large that it will dominate the youth group program? Will those who aren't in that program feel left out?

3. How can we tell if the program should be discontinued? (One of the greatest flaws of a successful program is that we can sometimes try to keep it going even after it has lost its effectiveness.)

4. How do we keep the group growing in spiritual depth?

5. To what extent should we develop the special ministry? Some groups do choir tours or the like; is that what we want? If so, how do we plan a tour? (Principles outlined in the next chapter will be helpful.)

Specialized ministry can be a dynamic part of the overall youth program because it gives students a special opportunity to serve others. Students learn that the purpose of the youth ministry is to strengthen their faith so that they in turn can strengthen others' faith. If they learn this principle—that we receive so that we may give—they will be well prepared to be servants throughout their Christian lives.

17.
SPECIAL MINISTRIES: MISSION OR SERVICE TEAMS

One of the most exciting developments in youth ministry over the past dozen years are youth mission teams. *Group* magazine workcamps, Teen Missions International, and Mountain T.O.P. (Tennessee Outreach Program) are but a few of the groups that organize youth service teams.

But what about planning such a trip just for your own youth group? Can it be done? My answer is a resounding yes. In fact, I believe that such workcamp experiences have been essential to our youth ministry's discipleship and leadership development (see appendix for "Mission Teams For Discipling Youth").

The Rationale

Mission teams not only serve poor people in our own nation and in third world nations, but the members of the team also learn invaluable lessons about human relationships. In addition to these reasons, we suggest three other reasons for designing mission teams for high school students.*

1. *Modeling.* Jesus' discipleship ministry might be summarized in the phrase "follow me." He built his ministry to his twelve chosen ones on the principle that experience is the best teacher. He never told them to do something that he didn't exemplify for them.

---

*We have taken junior high students on mission trips, but with varied results. If a junior high service team is designed, keep in mind the special needs of junior high students (see chapter 14) and learn from those who have experience with junior high teams.

Mission teams for young people are an excellent opportunity for modeling. The older adults who lead the team and the missionaries who work with the team have unparalleled opportunity to model both the Christian life and Christian compassion for others. Such modeling leaves lasting impressions on the spirits and hearts of the student participants.

2. *Memories.* In his book *Is There Life After High School?* Ralph Keyes suggests that the high school experience is the most important period of time for forming memories. If this is true, youth leaders in the local church need to work hard to build an environment in the youth group where positive memories can be formed.[1]

When we design a team, we hope that it will provide positive memories. And our students have verified that this is exactly what happens: when they apply for college, many of our students list the youth missionary teams as *the most important and memorable experience* of their high school life. That kind of testimony encourages us to make these teams a priority in the youth ministry.

3. *Missionaries.* The 1980 Conference in World Evangelism in Pattaya, Thailand, set a goal for 200,000 new missionaries by the year 2000. What an incredible goal! Yet how can it be achieved?

Many mission leaders believe this goal will be fulfilled by people who are now in high school. Reaching and influencing those young people, then, is part of global mission strategy. In his book *Student Power in World Missions* David Howard says, "When students decide to act, things happen. That is the history of missions. For the missionary movement has had a tremendous vitality often sparked by students with a worldwide vision."[2]

The primary goal of youth mission teams is to plant within the students seeds of desire that will help them grow into cross-cultural servants of Jesus Christ. By exposing high school students to the goals, visions, and experiences of mission life, we can influence them as they make plans for their further education and careers.

We have seen that happen in the years we have been involved

---

[1] Ralph Keyes, *Is There Life After High School?*, (New York, NY: Warner Books, 1976).

[2] David Howard, *Student Power in World Missions*, (Downers Grove, IL: InterVarsity Press, 1979), back copy.

in youth mission teams. Students from our mission teams have become or are preparing to become foreign missionaries, missionary pilots, urban ministers, refugee camp workers, and people who shape international laws that influence the poor. Many of these students testify that their initial desire to serve God in these capacities began in their youth mission experiences. Other students, whose careers are not related to mission work, have developed deep sensitivities to the needs of mission workers and the needs of the poor. These people will influence mission work in other ways: serving on church mission boards, financially supporting mission work, hosting international students who study in this country, and advocating for the poor in our cities.

PLANNING A MISSION TEAM

Before you even begin to plan, form a small group who will pray and brainstorm with you. Having a group of people to share in the planning, development, and leadership stages of a project will ease the burden on everyone. Although a successful youth project will be a consolidated team effort, the bulk of the planning will be done by the youth leader(s). The time needed to plan a project will vary with the nature of the project, of course, but we suggest beginning at least eight or twelve months in advance. Part-time or volunteer youth leaders may need even more time to prepare.

Step One: Decide What You Want

After learning about our youth missions program, many youth leaders want to start similar programs for their groups. However, the plans that work for us may not work for other groups. Each group needs to formulate its own plan to meet the goals, abilities, and financial needs of its unique group. Use the following questions to help you decide what your particular group needs/wants:

1. *What are your objectives?* Do you want to build your leadership? Will you work only with students who are interested in missions? Do you want to give cross-cultural exposure or simply exposure to serving others?

One of our principal objectives each year is to give students first-hand experience in urban, rural, and international settings.

This objective determines where we will go and who will go with us.

2. *Where will you go?* How far can you travel? Can you afford to fly? Does the church have a van that you can use? Where are your contacts?

3. *What type of work can your group do?* Painting? Construction? Evangelism? Teaching Bible school?

4. *How long will you go?* One week? Two weeks? All summer? The fact that most young people need to get jobs will affect how long you can go. Also many leaders may have to sacrifice vacation time to accompany the team. Be realistic.

5. *When do you want to go?* During school vacations? Over the summer? Can you travel midweek and save on airfare?

6. *How much can your group afford?* The socio-economic background of your church and your students will determine where you can go. Be cautious and sensitive not to shoot too high. Offering a project that is out of the financial reach of the families of your church could discourage your students from missionary service.

7. *What will you offer the people for whom you work?* Will you pay for your own food? How about lodging? Such questions should be answered before you approach missionaries about working with them. Our policy has always been that we will pay for our food, our travel, and at least part of the cost of our supplies. We expect the hosts to arrange for our lodging and to arrange for food preparation.

Step Two: Look for Opportunities

After deciding what you are looking for, begin pursuing opportunities. Some of the most obvious options are the missionaries supported by your own church family. You also might contact friends or pastors from other churches in your denomination.

Don't expect all responses to be positive, however. Some mission organizations are hesitant to do projects with high school students. We have found that one fifth of our contacts result in actual projects. However, once you have built up a good reputation, recommendations from missions groups will lend credibility to your work for future projects.

Undergird your search for opportunities with both prayer and expectancy. Several years ago we had received several rejection letters for projects we had hoped to establish. Although we were discouraged, we continued to pray that God would open doors for us. During that time of apparent closed doors, I visited a travel agency on some personal business. There I met a man who was a missionary in Central America. As we talked, I casually mentioned our desire to send a summer team to work in Central America. His interest blossomed into an eventual open door for fifteen students to serve in Costa Rica.

Step Three: Recruit Leaders

The most basic question for planning mission teams is often this: who will lead the team? Project opportunities and enthusiastic high school students are of no use without adults to lead the team.

Go first to your church people who are interested in mission work. Members of the missionary committee are often the best prospects because even if they aren't personally interested or able to become leaders, they may know people who are.

Try to recruit at least one adult for every four students. Young couples or singles are some of the best possibilities because they'll more easily keep pace with the high school metabolism. Try to find leaders who are willing to stay with the students on the projects; couples who insist on private quarters may not be able to relate as effectively to the students.

Try to get early commitments from leaders. Not only will this allow you to build a more effective leadership team, but it also will give leaders adequate time to get to know the students. Few people can develop quality relationships with students on a one-week or three-week project. The most effective mission teams are those whose leaders have long-term relationships with the students.

DEVELOPING A MISSION TEAM

While the planning stage sometimes overlaps with the developing stage, the development phase sees the momentum build and the project beginning to fall together. During this stage, excitement builds in both the youth group and in the church family.

Step One: Planning the Budget and Raising Money

How much will it cost? Before approaching the students, parents, or missions committee with the project, the youth leader must have an idea of project costs. Every project will differ, but the main costs include

- travel (tolls, gasoline, air travel, land travel, visa charges, etc.)
- food (both on-site and travel costs)
- lodging (both on-site and travel costs)
- supplies (paint, cement, etc.)

Students should be held responsible for their own passports, spending money, film, and clothing costs.

The following principles and ideas have helped form our policies in budgeting and fund raising.

1. When presenting the proposed project to your missions committee, be generous in your estimates of expenses; the price of travel, gasoline, and food, for instance, may increase, and you don't want to underestimate your costs.

2. Ask the missions committee to provide funds for certain aspects of the project like supplies and scholarship aid.

3. Make sure students aren't "given" the trip. One of the most growing experiences for teenagers is trusting God to provide the needed money. We instruct parents to donate only a portion of the student's cost. The student is then responsible to trust God for the rest. The students either must earn the money or must apply for scholarship aid.

4. Make allowances for leaders. It's too much to expect people to give up vacation time, lead a youth team, and then pay full price for the trip. First decide how much leaders will pay, and then decide how the balance of the money will be provided. Will the leaders' expenses be factored into the students' costs? Will the missions committee supply the balance of the leaders' expenses?

5. Give students and parents additional information about

other sources of funds. Some people in the church or some organizations may provide funds for student aid, and this can be part of the fund-raising procedure.

Step Two: Promotion

Early in the development stage, begin promoting the youth mission team idea to the youth, their parents, and the church. Promotion might include bulletin announcements, general informational brochures, and posters that will generate interest from the church family.

The purpose of promotion is to get people interested and thinking about a project. This is the time to ask students, "Who would like to consider working in the inner city next summer?" or "How would you like to serve in Appalachia?"

Begin promotion about four to eight months before the targeted date of the project. In the beginning, use words like "we may" or "we hope to," avoiding promises that may not be fulfilled.

Step Three: Recruitment

The recruitment phase begins when you have decided to proceed with the project. This is the time for the presentation of the *exact* details—how much, how long, when, how many, where, and what will be the task.

The recruiting process is often difficult because the young people may be hesitant to commit themselves, especially to a new idea like a youth mission team. It is wise to have the support of the other youth leaders (or sponsors), the parents, and especially the pastor. If the pastor endorses what the youth leader is trying to do, it will increase the credibility of such a project to the church family.

The following guidelines may help accelerate the recruiting process:

1. Inform people of as many details as possible. People fear the unknown, and announcement of the facts will answer many questions before they are asked.

2. Emphasize commitment. Nonrefundable deposits, official applications, official letters of acceptance, and a published list of

requirements are a few ways to help students realize that they are committing themselves to serious work.

3. Give personal attention to interested people. Such attention is often an affirmation to the student, serving to calm his/her fears and answer the doubt, "I don't know if I could do it."

4. Emphasize limits and deadlines. Limiting the size of the mission team will motivate the students to register early. A registration deadline (and possibly a penalty fee) also will force decisions.

Step Four: Requirements

Gerry Hartis, director of a stress camping program, summarizes his approach to camping as "No pain, no gain." The best in life will always cost us.

High school students are aware of this principle. They know that if a program demands little of them, it must be worth little. For this reason, preparatory requirements are important to the students who are considering a youth missionary team.

We use our requirements to help us screen student applicants in several ways. First, we want to challenge students to apply for the teams, but we don't want them to think of the project as a vacation; we want them to *know* that hard work lies ahead. Second, we train our students rigorously because we want to bring them together as a team *before* they go so that they will do a better job on the project. Third, we use these requirements to enable us to predict problems that may arise. We don't want to drive 1000 miles or fly 10,000 miles just to find out that two students aren't hard workers. Finally, we use our requirements to foreshadow the rigors of missionary training. From fund raising to the red tape of application forms, from the pain of shots to the anxiety of interviews, we try to use these team requirements to simulate what it is like to prepare to be a missionary.

We have found a direct correlation between the rigor of the requirements and the successful accomplishment of the team. The summer that we tightened our requirements to the point of being excessive, we had more applicants than we had ever had before. It seemed that when students saw the requirements, they knew that these teams were a great challenge, and they accepted the challenge.

The requirements we make for students and leaders aren't original. We combine concepts from the training programs of Teen Missions International and the Wilderness Educational Services of Gordon-Conwell Theological Seminary. We also use a training manual—an idea we borrowed from the Youth Evangelism Explosion program of the Coral Ridge Presbyterian Church of Fort Lauderdale, Florida.

The requirements that have worked so well for us in preparing our youth mission teams include two categories: personal preparation and team preparation.

Personal Preparation

1. *Application forms.* We ask our students to answer questions like, "How do you know you're a Christian?" and "What are the strengths/weaknesses that you will bring to your team?" We also require them to furnish references: two from other students who can describe the applicant's witness at high school and one from an adult who can attest to the applicant's ability to work.

2. *Writing assignments.* After a person has been accepted to the team, he or she is given writing assignments that may include a book report on a missionary biography or a geographical report that explores the culture, religions, climate, or languages of the area in which their team will serve. Students are expected to do one-page reports that are neat enough to be photocopied; when all reports are collected, each team member receives a copy of each report.

3. *Fund raising.* Each participant is responsible for his or her own finances. This includes a fifty-dollar deposit paid two or three months before the team leaves and the rest paid six weeks before the team leaves. Students who need aid are encouraged to write letters to friends and relatives or to apply for aid from our church's international missions committee. Students who apply for committee aid usually receive it, but only after they complete another book report and appear before the committee for a personal interview (which can be an intimidating experience for a teenager).

4. *Prayer support.* Each student and leader is required to

recruit at least three prayer supporters (only two of whom may be from his or her home). This requirement allows students to sense the personal encouragement of others in the church. It's also an important way to include students who aren't able to go on a team; a student prayer supporter feels more involved with the project, even if he or she can't go.

5. *Other preparations.* These may include getting the needed shots or passport (if necessary), acquiring personal spending money, completing "Parent Permission Forms," and participating in required team events (below).

Team Preparation

We have required the personal preparations for many years, but only in the last few have we worked to prepare the team as a unit. Team preparation requires the teams to be selected at least two months before they are scheduled to depart.

1. *The team retreat.* The team retreat is our most effective tool to prepare our teams. Fashioned after Teen Missions International's "Boot Camp," the retreat includes work together as a team, intra team competitions, an obstacle course, and many hours of team interaction and training. The team retreat isn't a cure-all; in fact, it causes problems to surface, permitting us to see and address them before our teams depart.

2. *The team covenant.* The team members prepare this document on the retreat. It is, in effect, a contract between group members, describing the Christian community that the team wants to build. The covenant contains four parts:

a. *Purpose statement.* Why does our team exist, and what type of people do we want to be?

b. *Goals.* What characteristics should we reflect if we are to fulfill our purpose?

c. *Structure.* Will we accomplish our goal through team meetings? leaders? dealing with conflict?

d. *Evaluation.* How do we evaluate and correct ourselves?

Drawing up a team covenant can be complicated, but from junior high students to young professionals, we have found that a covenant works in keeping the team together, in helping them

177

resolve conflicts, and in giving them a sense of qualitative accomplishment as a team.

3. *Team meetings.* We require three or four other meetings to give out information, to address parents, and to answer questions. Team meetings also give the team time to pray together, building a spiritual foundation for the experiences ahead of them.

4. *The team notebook.* Each team member receives an orientation notebook that includes instructions on cross-cultural adaptation, training about functioning as a team, and space for other orientation information. We have found that this official notebook creates a seriousness about the project and a positive sense of professionalism.

5. *The team commissioning:* The church sets aside an entire evening service to commission the teams. The team reports on the work that it will do; team members recite the team memory verses; the pastor preaches on servanthood; and at the end of the service, the team members kneel at the front of the sanctuary while the elders and pastors lay hands on them and pray for them. We require team participation in this service because it communicates a sense of church-wide support for the work that will be undertaken.

Step Five: Training the Leaders

Experience has taught us that the relative success or failure of a youth mission team is directly dependent on the leadership. The adult leaders are the glue that holds the team together. For this reason, their training is essential in preparing for a mission team.

We review relational issues with the leaders, discussing how to deal with crises, how to handle the complainer, how to encourage communication, how to listen, and how to promote a healthy team spirit. We discuss practical matters: what to pack, how to go through customs, and how to manage trip finances. In addition, the leaders should be skilled in whatever activity the team will do at the project site; if the team is to paint, the leaders should be skilled at painting as well as teaching teenagers how to paint.

Consider using special speakers or instructors. An expert in small group dynamics, an experienced travel agent, or a building or painting contractor can also give valuable training to the leaders.

Step Six: Practical Details

While students and leaders are in training for their responsibilities, it's easy for the team leader to think everything is going well. However, dozens of other logistical details have to be worked out in the few months before the project begins.

1. *Travel details.* For a local trip, travel details include arranging for cars or a van, mapping out the routes, and arranging for lodging, if overnight travel is necessary.

For an international trip or any trip that requires flying, the travel details are more extensive. Ordering tickets, getting visas or visitor cards, making sure students have passports and necessary shots, and staying in touch with the travel agency require organization and diligence.

2. *Host details.* It is important to maintain consistent communication with the people at the project site. Letters and phone calls not only help you inform them about your plans but they also can help you learn more about the culture, climate, and situation into which you are going. Ask the host group for advice about the clothes the group will need, which shots are required, the cheapest means of travel, etc.

3. *Financial details.* Once expenses have been calculated, collect money from the team members. It's important to collect the money well in advance of the departure date so that money is available to pay for advance-purchase plane tickets (the least expensive way to travel by air), to send checks ahead for food and lodging, and to insure students' commitment to the project. Early collection also will allow for proper ordering of needed checks (without putting personal or church accounts into deficit) and early purchasing of travelers checks needed for the trip. We suggest collecting money at least six weeks in advance for projects that require air travel and at least thirty days in advance for projects that require only land travel.

Our policy is to pay all team travel expenses by traveler's checks carried by the leaders. For example, when the team eats lunch during a trip, the team leaders use a traveler's check to pay for the entire team.

Explore your options for insurance coverage. We suggest two

possibilities: either ask the church to cover the team (through its existing policy or, if necessary, through an added rider) or ask each team member to provide his or her own coverage. Whatever the choice, have something *in writing* for each person—and his or her parents—before you depart.

Step Seven: Building Church Awareness

One of the church's most important functions in developing a youth mission team is affirmation. It's the members of the church family who give the youth the special sense of being "sent out" in service. The best affirmation comes when the church is fully aware of the project and of the specific people involved. Building this awareness is an essential part of the development phase.

Every church has a different organizational setup, so the means of building this awareness will differ from congregation to congregation. Every church, however, has some general publication (like the weekly bulletin) that can inform the church about the youth mission team. Information about the project and the team members should appear often as the departure date gets closer.

Perhaps the most important way to build awareness is the commissioning service described earlier. This commissioning service gives the congregation an opportunity to see the entire team, to hear about the project, to listen to their expectations of the trip, to share their excitement, and to catch their vision. The purpose of the commissioning service is not only to inform the church but also to build the students' sense of representing the church in their mission.

Step Eight: Planning for Pictures

Before the team leaves, discuss how you will tell about your experiences when you return home from the project. Although it may seem overwhelming to discuss these details in the midst of all the pre-trip planning, thinking ahead will help you return with the kind of pictures you'll need for presentations to the church and other groups.

We assign at least two people as team photographers. The photographers should know ahead of time what kinds of pictures they will need to take. Try to take pictures that show the project itself (if your project is painting buildings on a mission site, "before and after" pictures demonstrate the team's accomplishment), the people on the project site, the culture of the project area, and the team's interaction with each other and with the people in the project. Choose photographers who will be sensitive to "pictures that tell a story": a slide of the young boy whose life was affected by the well the group helped to dig in Haiti will help you tell that story when you return home from the project.

We ask our photographers to take two or three pictures of the same sight, insuring that we will have at least one good picture to use in our presentations. We take only slides because they are less expensive and can be processed into prints if we need them.

LEADING A MISSION TEAM

On the day of departure, meet with the team members and their families at a central location. Use this farewell time to pray together for the team and the trip that lies ahead. Your pastor or an elder may want to be with you to commission the group once again.

Step One: As You Travel

The travel experience may be the most significant time to build anticipation of the upcoming work and service. While traveling to (or from) a service area, emphasize

1. *Team pride.* The way a team dresses will influence how they feel about themselves and how they will behave. In 1980, we began asking the men to wear coats and ties and the women to wear dresses or skirts. While many complained about this requirement in the beginning, they realized later that it built a comradery between team members, and it made them feel proud of how they looked as a team.

2. *Team witness.* The excitement of travel sometimes causes students to forget the Lord whom they serve. For this reason, the leaders should emphasize that the team's behavior, attitudes, and language will be a witness for (or against) the glory of Christ to fellow travelers and other people that the team encounters.

3. *Team courtesy.* Remind team members to be courteous to

181

gas station attendants, flight attendants, or food service workers. Courtesy should also be shown to other team members; remind team members to help each other with baggage and to look out for each other's needs. These attitudes of thoughtfulness and kindness may be the team's only witness to the people whom they encounter.

Step Two: After You Arrive

After you arrive, you'll need time to adjust. New people, new surroundings, and in some cases a new language or culture will take some getting used to. Be patient.

1. *The leaders' example.* In the beginning, students will watch leaders for their responses to the new setting. Leaders must realize that their actions become models for the students' behavior. During the initial days, leaders will fulfill three important roles:

a. *Counselors.* Through careful listening, leaders will learn which team members need encouragement, comfort, or correcting. Leaders will need to spend extra time with those students.

b. *Pacesetters.* If the leaders are excited about the people, the culture, and the joy of discovery, the students will follow. Setting the pace also requires that the leaders work the hardest and pray the most often. Leaders will need to slow down the students whose zeal is greater than their ability and to prod the students who seem to be lazy.

c. *Mediators.* The leaders will mediate not only between members of the team but also between the team and the host group. Inevitably, team members will get on each other's nerves, and bitterness will arise. Leaders should help reconcile the differences between team members. It's rare for a team to work together for several weeks without every team member (including the leaders) having to ask another for forgiveness at one time or another.

As mediator between the team and the hosts, the leaders must speak up if the team is being worked too hard. The team members are servants, but they shouldn't be abused.

The leaders also need to interact with the hosts about other issues. For instance, one of our host groups assumed that our team was very wealthy. The host took us on one tour after another, out to lunch, and then by boat to a high-class beach. In two days, he expended almost our entire discretionary budget. The leaders met with him and told him that we preferred choosing how to spend our money. It ruffled the missionary a bit, but our relationship with him was smoother for the rest of the project.

2. *Student exposure.* Students will learn best when they are exposed to as many aspects of the experience as possible.

a. *Hosts.* When the team members have first-hand experience with missionaries and local or national leaders (and their families), the students will discover that these servants of Christ are normal people who hurt, get discouraged, yet triumph in Christ.

b. *Culture.* Seeing other cultures helps students evaluate their own cultural background. At first they may think that people look "funny" or that people drive on "the wrong side of the road." Leaders should help them see some of their reactions as cultural biases. Cultural exposure will be the best way for students to learn that cultures and people can differ without being "right" or "wrong."

c. *Hard work.* Many high school students (especially those in ninth or tenth grade) will not have worked an eight-hour day or a forty-hour week. Diligent teamwork will stretch students and teach them that they can work harder than they ever thought possible. Reminding them that they are there to serve Jesus will provide some of the needed motivation.

d. *Leaders.* Most students will not have lived with an older Christian person (other than their parents) for any significant length of time. Living with, watching, and emulating the leaders will be the best training in discipleship that some students will ever receive. (See appendix for article on "Mission Teams for Discipling Youth.")

Step Three: Work and Play

The two most important facets of a mission/service project are the work and the play. Because most of the waking moments of the project will be spent in one of these two functions, it is important to make the maximum use of this time. To make the entire experience a learning adventure, consider these issues.

1. *Plan for measurable results.* High school students are

pragmatists; they think practically rather than conceptually. For this reason, measurable results will be the most positive way for them to know that God has used them in his service. Although the students' presence and enthusiasm will be a great encouragement to those for whom they work, this will not register in the students' mind as a measure that God used their lives. They prefer to see some project completed, some wall built, or some house painted.

The desire to produce measurable results should be tempered by the resources and abilities of the team. The decision about what projects will be completed should be set *after* you arrive on the job and start working. Setting a goal to finish painting a house—only to be detained by inclement weather or limited supplies—will only confirm in the students' minds that God did *not* use them. Sometimes it's best *not* to set definite goals and to be satisfied with whatever you are able to complete.

2. *The leaders' excitement.* Because high school students are often inhibited in front of each other, they will hesitate to show enthusiasm or excitement at a new discovery. A high school guy will usually hesitate to register excitement over a beautiful flower or a colorful butterfly. If the leaders show uninhibited excitement about different experiences during the project, the students will experience greater freedom to learn, discover, and enjoy themselves and their surroundings.

3. *The journal.* Although teenagers are impressionable, they don't always remember their impressions. Recommending or requiring daily journal entries helps students to articulate what they have learned. This writing and recording will fix the experiences in the students' minds long after the project is over. They may want to use their journals to record the most significant experiences of each day, or you may want to give specific questions for them to answer in their journal. After having met one of the church leaders in the third world country they are visiting, they could respond to these questions: How is God using pastor Nuogo? How is his ministry different from your pastor's ministry? What godly characteristics do you see in his life? What can you learn from him?

4. *Fun activities.* When missionaries report back to supporting churches, they sometimes give the impression that all they do is

work. While this may be true for some missionaries, it isn't true for all.

Most people, no matter what type of cultural setting they live in, have some sort of recreation. To give the students on the youth service team a full experience, make sure they spend time swimming in a stream, hiking a mountain, feeding wild deer, or snorkeling on a coral reef. Whatever it is, make sure to include it during the project.

We recommend including an entire day of fun at the end of the project. This does three things: it gives students a goal to aim for; it gives them a sense of reward for work well done; and it finishes the project with a positive impression.

Step Four: Feedback

During the project, the most crucial relational tool needed to keep the operation running smoothly is feedback. The students and the leaders need time to talk together.

1. *Talking together helps the team deal with disappointments.* One of our teams went to Alberta, Canada, expecting dog teams and scenes from Jack London novels. Instead, they found expansive plains and oil derricks. As a team they needed time together—apart from their hosts—to voice their disappointments and to decide together to work at overcoming these feelings of disappointment.

2. *Talking together allows time to cope with problems or complaints.* The mediatorial role of the leader comes into play here. Allowing for feedback will help leaders find out what things are bothering the team members.

3. *Talking together allows the team to let down.* Because the students come from a certain culture, they will see or hear things that will seem odd or silly to them. Team feedback time allows students time to work through their reactions without hurting the feelings of the hosts or embarrassing the team.

4. *Talking together allows for confrontations.* Sometimes one or two people will need to be exhorted for being too lazy or too secretive. Other times those who are ill or tired will need

encouragement. Team feedback time is the most appropriate time for these confrontations.

Step Five: After the Trip

The most difficult adjustment for most students (and leaders) will occur after the trip is over. From an intense, highly growth-oriented, deeply spiritual time, the students will separate and return home to life as usual.

One girl returned home after two weeks in South America. After an hour or more of reporting on her first experiences in a Latin culture, she knew that her parents weren't understanding. All that her mother could say was, "Well, the weather was hot while you were gone." The girl was crushed.

Upon returning, some students will feel extremely lonely, thinking that they are misunderstood by their family or friends. They will wonder if the experience was just a dream. They will question why no one is as excited about this trip as they are.

Others will experience a spiritual letdown after the trip because of the sudden removal of intimate fellowship. Still others may be emotionally affected, even depressed.

To deal with these problems, consider the following:

1. *Deprogramming.* Shortly after the trip is over, schedule a reunion. Only in their own group will they find others who are as excited as they are. Deprogramming times should include an honest discussion about the real problems that they face now that they are home. Confronting the problems directly will help students resolve the issues.

2. *Affirmations.* A variety of sessions should be planned to help students feel a sense of the affirmation of the church family who sent them out earlier. Meeting with the missions committee, the pastor, and the entire church body will enable students to report what they have learned. It will also re-confirm to students the special quality of the work they accomplished.

Step Six: Follow-up

The effects of these projects will be felt long after the project is over. Assuming that one of the goals of the project is to stimulate missions interest in students, careful follow-up of the team members (both leaders and students) will help maintain that interest.

Follow-up can be done in a variety of ways. We suggest two possibilities:

The missions committee may want to follow up the team members. Each person on the missions committee can be responsible to pray for, befriend, and reach out to a few students who were on mission teams. Even after the students leave the church, the committee members can continue to encourage and support the students' interest in missions.

"Trophies" can also be used to help maintain students' interest. Displaying a team picture in the church lobby or awarding T-shirts that announce "I painted a house for Jesus" will act as further expressions of the church family's affirmation of these students.

EPILOGUE: THE END RESULTS

It would be nice to say that hundreds of the students and leaders who have participated in our projects are now pursuing missionary service. But that isn't the case. However, even though only some of our former team members are in active missionary service, the others have benefited in several significant ways:

1. A greater understanding of servanthood.

2. An experience of and a desire for teamwork.

3. An increased world awareness—specifically, a better perspective on their own church and own problems because they understand that the world and God's people are larger and more varied than they had known before.

4. An intensified desire to pursue God's will for their lives.

5. An increased willingness to consider missionary service. The most significant outcome is that participants on these teams have a new perspective of missionary service. Rather than considering the call to missions as extraordinary or as a special call to a few spiritual giants, our students look at missionary service as a *normal* option to consider for their future.

As a final note, consider Jesus' command in Matthew 9: "Pray therefore the Lord of the harvest to send out laborers into his harvest" (Matt. 9:38 RSV). The harvest is plentiful, and the best possible outcome of youth mission teams is more laborers. But the priority is still *prayer*. The harvest field, the laborers, and the fruits all belong to the Lord.

"BUT WHAT DO I DO WHEN. . . ?" (CONTINGENCY PLANS)

A chapter like this often can give the mistaken impression that projects are problem free and that leaders will breeze through the weeks of a youth service project without an obstacle. This isn't true. Problems will come.

The problems listed below vary widely in severity, but they have all occurred at one time or another on our teams. Be sure to read both the problem and the solution because some of the solutions are preventative and are designed to keep the problem from occurring.

The first way to respond to any problem is to pray. Ask God for the needed help and wisdom. Pray together with other members of the leadership team. Then select from the leadership team the person most equipped to handle the problem.

1. *Problem: paranoid parents.* Parents are insecure because you are taking their children to Bula-Bula land, and they are especially worried because *you* are the leader.

Solutions: While the problem can't be totally eliminated, it can be alleviated by the following actions:

a. Meet with the parents to discuss your plans and goals for the project.

b. Give the parents a copy of the team itinerary, your host's phone number, and your plans for safety on the project.

c. Call the church while you are on the project to let people know that you are safe.

d. Have some objective person (your pastor or other church leader) reassure the parents of your competence and the competence of the students. Protective, well-meaning parents often need to be reminded of the fact that their children are growing up and can handle responsibility.

2. *Problem: shots and passports.* You don't know which shots are required and how to get passports.

Solutions: Ask the team members to get tetanus shots, regardless of the location of the project. This is a safety measure against simple cuts that may occur. Information about shots needed for overseas travel can be obtained from your hosts, travel agent, and the state or federal health boards. International vaccination booklets are available at the local public health office, and passport applications are available at your post office.

3. *Problem: no funds.* You have an opportunity to do a project, but you need financial aid for the team. You ask the church's missions committee, but either they have no aid available or they aren't sure that this project is a good idea.

Solutions: Lack of financial resources is a common problem in planning a mission team. Lack of enthusiastic support is also common. You may need to have one or two successful projects before the church offers its full support. Consider alternatives. First pray, then pursue other options:

a. Ask organizations within the church or the community for assistance. The church's women's fellowship or some community group may be willing to undertake your team as a special project.

b. Raise funds by sponsoring a car wash, a bake sale, etc. at the church. Doing these projects together is an excellent way to built team unity and comradery.

c. Plan for and announce youth projects a long time in advance so that students can request gifts of money at Christmas, graduation, or birthdays.

4. *Problem: travel problems.* Your van breaks down; you lose some luggage; a flight is cancelled; you miss a connection; a ticket or travelers checks are lost.

Solutions: Some of these problems can be prevented with appropriate planning. To get out of these predicaments, use these resources:

a. Carry with you important phone numbers: the company from which you rented the van, the airlines, friends that you know along your route, the travelers checks offices, and the United States consulate.

b. In the airport, ask questions of the flight attendants or desk agents, who are usually kind and helpful in giving travel advice.

c. Read a book on "traveler's rights" before you go. Airlines have certain obligations to fulfill and certain standards for quality of service. Knowing your rights will help you locate luggage, get booked on another flight, or respond to an emergency.

d. Before you leave, give someone at home your itinerary, the route you plan to travel, your ticket numbers, and your travelers checks numbers. If something is lost (or if you get lost), then you can call this person for help.

e. To avoid losing tickets, money, or valuables, carry these on your person while traveling. While you are on site at your project, arrange to have these items stored in a safe.

5. *Problem: on-site difficulties.* Your host spends too much money; someone on the teams gets sick or hurt; someone is a discipline problem or a lazy worker; the host overworks the team.

Solutions: Many of these problems can be avoided by accurate communication *before* the trip. Communication with your host should include the *exact* amount of money you will be sending ahead for supplies and food. If the host seems hesitant to accept this amount, inform him or her that this is the maximum and that anything over it must come from another source.

Communication with the team before the trip should identify the workers who may be lazy or discipline problems. Team requirements and training meetings or fund-raising efforts should help the leader identify and address the problem worker.

Within twenty-four hours after your team arrives, go over the itinerary for the project with your host. Tell the host how many days you hope to work and how many days you hope to relax or tour. All work and no play may get more work done, but it will disillusion students and staff about mission service. For a two-week team, plan for one or two days of rest or vacation. Don't include the days of worship and church activity in these two; speaking at churches will be a wonderful experience, but it will not be restful.

6. *Problem: health.* Work can't be accomplished if team members are ill.

Solutions: Preventative measures can help team members maintain good health.

a. Upon arrival, find out the location of the first-aid kit, the nearest doctor, and the nearest clinic or hospital with emergency capabilities.

b. Be prepared for and sensitive to the menstrual cycles of the women on the team. Most women will be slowed by the onset of their period, so be sensitive. Female leaders can help teenaged girls on the team.

c. Expect diarrhea. Even the local projects introduce team members to unfamiliar food or water that may upset their digestive tracts. On the international projects, diarrhea is almost guaranteed.

To minimize this problem, ask the host what is safe to eat and drink (just remember that in foreign countries what is safe for the host may not be safe for you; the hosts' bodies may have developed immunities to germs that may make you violently ill.). If the water is unsafe to drink unless it is boiled, make sure all team members are careful not to drink unboiled water or use ice cubes made from unboiled water. Also be careful not to eat raw vegetables, like lettuce, that may be washed in unboiled water. Water filter cups or purification tablets may be obtained before leaving on the project, and a doctor may be able to give you a prescription for Lomotil or Parapectolin, both helpful anti-diarrheals. Pepto-Bismol or some other antacid are also helpful for stomach disorders.

18.
ORGANIZING FOR PARENTAL SUPPORT

For many of us, the idea of parental support in youth ministry is frightening. Demanding parents who expect us to mend the rift between them and their children make us nervous. Parents who welcome us to the youth group with "Let's see how long you will last!" send chills down our spines. Grateful parents who state, "I'm so glad you are the leader; I am confident that you can help my Johnny," remind us that some parents hope we'll be miracle workers.

Excessive demands. Unrealistic expectations. Unjustified criticisms. All these things keep us from wanting to work with parents—but we must.

If our desire is for more than a "fun-and-games" youth ministry, if we hope for long-term effects in the lives of youth, and if we truly desire to minister to young people, we must get the parents to help us. As we observed in an earlier chapter, it is parents' values, attitudes, and relationships that will have the greatest long-term effect on youth. To build our youth ministries without concern for the parents is to neglect the most influential people in our students' lives. When we realize that our efforts in youth ministry complement (or, in some cases, contradict) the foundations built in the home, we begin to understand our need to get parental support.

GAINING PARENTAL SUPPORT
Through the years, I have come to realize that parents will offer their support if we adequately present ourselves. The

following principles can help guide us in our relationships to parents:

Commit Ourselves to Young People

Parents want to know that we have their children's best interests in mind, that we are advocates for their children. For this reason, a long-term commitment to youth ministry is one of the best bases on which trust can be built with the parents because they see that we are deeply committed to helping teenagers grow and mature into full, responsible adults.

Communicate with Parents

If we are secretive about the youth ministry or the program, parents will get suspicious. We must let them know what's happening in the youth group. We also must communicate to parents that we are willing to listen to them; ignoring their wisdom and experience will cause us to sacrifice a great many insights into working with youth.

Share Resources with Parents

In many cases, parents are out of touch with the teenage world. When we offer some observations, parents usually listen. The effective youth leader realizes, "Hey, I do know something about today's teenager, and parents could benefit from what I know."

To share resources with parents, our ministry offers parent seminars (ninety minutes) every other month. We have addressed teenage music, peer pressure, sexual activity, handling money, and financing a college education. Each seminar includes a time for questions as well as a time for presenting other related books and resources.

One of the greatest resources is other parents. Opening doors of communication among parents of teenagers helps them to share their wisdom, give support to each other, and recognize that they aren't alone in their problems.

Be Sensitive To Parents' Needs

Parents' critical words or high expectations often are caused by one basic problem: Parents see themselves as failing, and unable to handle the guilt alone, they blame the youth leader, pastor, school teachers, or anyone else who happens to be around.

It's difficult for those of us without teenage children to imagine the pressures and fears parents experience as their children grow up. Some handle it well; others crack under the load. John White describes the home where crisis is occurring:

> Storms of unbelievable ferocity can turn homes into disaster areas. In some households the emotional climate is rarely free from weather warnings. Instead of the gentleness and kindness that ought to prevail, bitterness, rage, resentment, and sorrow sweep through the household. In the wake of each storm, though calm may seem to dominate, stormy passions continue to rage inside the hearts of individual family members.[1]

The youth leader who aspires to win the support of parents must be willing and prepared to be a sounding board, a counselor, or a support to parents who are in great pain.

Sensitivity to parents' needs also may mean being cautious with our youth activity schedule: Parents are appreciative when we don't over-schedule (and take their children away from home too often), when we schedule meetings at times that are sensitive to family mealtimes, and when we schedule activity well in advance (especially in the summer so that family vacations can be planned).

Support the Family Unit

The youth leader who always sides with students against parents will fail. Promoting an "us vs. them" mentality is destructive.

Supporting the family unit means that we don't believe every word from our teenagers. One girl complained that her mother "beat" her. In a world of serious child abuse, I was concerned. I realized, however, that this sixteen year old was quite capable of exaggerating. With a few more questions, I learned that the mother

[1] John White, *Parents in Pain*, (Downers Grove, IL: InterVarsity Press, 1979), 77.

had slapped the girl—once—in response to a sassy, profane outburst. I was glad that I hadn't overreacted to the girl's initial story.

Supporting the family unit also means that we encourage young people to be obedient. When the whole youth group wants to go to a movie, but one parents says "no" to his or her teenager, our response is important. We must—if we are to promote family harmony—support the decisions of the parents even if we don't always agree.

We can also support the family unit by letting the youth group members know our spouses and children. Our influence as husband or wife and parent will be more effective when the young people see us interact in a family setting.

Respond Firmly to Parents

Parents need us to be realistic. A friend of mine accepted a position as a youth minister in a church that had many disillusioned "church kids." In his first month, he met with the parents. "I am here to do my best under God," he told them, "but I am not a miracle worker. If you want someone who can work miracles with your teenagers in a few short months, you have hired the wrong person." Although some parents were shocked at his candor, they understood exactly what he was saying (he has stayed at that church for four years, and by God's grace, he *has* "worked some miracles").

Be realistic when parents come to us with hard problems they are facing. They don't need a glib "God will work it all out" from us when they are experiencing a disaster. They are saying, "Look, we are in deep trouble; can you help at all?"

We can help parents keep their perspective. Some feel that they are "the only ones who have ever experienced this problem," and we need to help them see that there are others in the same predicament. We are also the ones who can reassure parents that they have not "wasted their lives" because their fifteen year old has started smoking.

Firm responses to parents also means challenging them about their own spiritual growth. I remind parents that their attitudes about God and church will be imitated by their teenagers. I tell them, "I will be challenging your teenagers to have a daily time to read the Bible, pray, and grow with God. I will encourage them to witness at school and at work and to pray for their friends. But I should tell you that these things rarely happen in the life of the young person if they aren't exemplified at home. For this reason, I urge you to be growing, witnessing, and living for Christ in your own life as the primary example to your teenagers."

Build Bridges Between Youth and Parents

In the Book of Ezekiel, God looks for someone who will "stand in the gap" between himself and the people, someone to be a bridge builder between those who are at odds with each other. Parents and young people need youth workers who will stand in the gap. Parents offer their support when they see us in that role, seeking to serve both them and their children.

Being bridge builders means that we teach parents how to understand their teenagers and the world in which they live. Being bridge builders also means that we openly challenge young people to love and care for their parents. Whether we encourage parents to visit the high school campus or whether we help teenagers write thank-you notes to their parents, building bridges requires work and creativity. Yet it's worth it. Strengthening the parent/child relationship will yield lifelong benefits.

Effectiveness in youth ministry means that we reach out to both students and parents. Drawing families together, teaching youth to be responsible as young adults and yet respectful as children, and helping parents to "let go" of their teenagers as they mature will not be easy. Nevertheless, we must practice these ways of gaining support from parents so that our youth ministries will be reaching those who have the maximum effect on teenagers—the parents.

PRACTICAL WAYS TO INVOLVE PARENTS

Perhaps some of us aren't so fearful of getting parental support as we are of getting parents involved. I don't mind telling parents about our "all-nighters," but to have them *involved* in the event (where they might pass judgment on my leadership and on the wisdom of my decisions) can be intimidating.

But remember that while support from parents is essential, their involvement is optional. In considering it, we can decide how involved we want them to be. Will we invite parents to an activity once a year or every week? Will they be on our staff team or just occasional guests?

If we want to have parents regularly involved, we must consider several issues. On the one hand, parental involvement can fill our need for adult leaders and can offer insight that can't be found in books. If many youth group members are from single-parent families, having parents regularly involved might meet a great need in their lives.

On the other hand, parental involvement can bring an element of discomfort for parents, their children in the group, and the youth leaders. The parents might feel overprotective, the young people cramped, and the youth leader caught within the tension. We must take the needs of the young people into account before we decide to involve parents regularly.

If we choose to have parents involved in the youth ministry, what will they do? Here are five roles parents can fill:

1. *Participants*. We can invite parents to come into the youth ministry in a friendly, non-authoritative role. Father/son or mother/daughter athletics, meals, or even cooperative service projects can build the relationships between teenagers and parents in a relatively nonthreatening environment.

2. *Leaders*. It's possible to have parents as youth leaders, if both parents and their children agree; however, parents need to allow their teenage children to be normal participants in the group.

3. *Occasional experts*. We can use parents as speakers and panel participants when discussing careers, college options, or even the problems of parenting.

4. *Advisers*. We have had parents serve on a parents' advisory board, which tells me how the youth group members are responding, which needs we are failing to meet, and how we can improve.

5. *Resources*. Parents can minister to each other, teaching,

counseling, or consoling each other. We can help this process by knowing which parents will be open and able to help others.

As we develop our sensitivity to the parents of teenagers, we can involve them more effectively so that students, parents, and families all benefit.

19.
ORGANIZING DISCIPLESHIP PROGRAMS

After graduating from college, I was asked to assume leadership in our church youth ministry. I was excited because I thought I could transfer the training I had received from Campus Crusade and the Navigators to high school students. My father, however, wasn't so excited. He thought that I was too "heavy" and that the discipleship training I had received was "over the teenagers' heads."

His observations raised some good questions: Can high school students be disciples? Are teenagers capable of maturing in their faith and following Jesus Christ? Instinctively, we all answer yes, but inwardly we may have my father's fears—that serious discipleship is too heavy or beyond the understanding of our youth.

But teenagers can be disciples! (It may be that some of Jesus' original twelve disciples were teenagers.) I have seen many young people excel in their relationships with the Lord and demonstrate full commitment to Jesus Christ. I believe in discipling young people.

Teenagers are able to make faith commitments that apply to their own lives. They can learn the disciplines of daily prayer, Bible reading, meditation, witnessing, and fellowship. Young people are wonderfully malleable in the hands of the Lord.

Our youth programs, however, may be the factor that determines whether or not our teenagers become disciples. If our youth activities and Bible lessons always are geared to the non-Christian student, our Christian students may find it difficult to grow beyond the point of being "baby" Christians. If we are always featuring "fun and games" but never offering "spiritual meat," we may be holding students back from their growth potential.

DISCIPLESHIP PROGRAMS

In order to maintain a balance between challenging the Christian students and reaching the non-Christians, we must have programs for students on various spiritual levels. For those who desire spiritual growth and discipleship, therefore, we must offer good training opportunities and discipleship programs.

The idea of discipleship "programs" is not a scriptural model. Jesus discipled his followers through his life. He didn't say, "Here is lesson #1; today we are going to talk about prayer." Instead, he took his disciples out to pray (or to watch him as he prayed). From their many days of concentrated time with Jesus, his disciples learned what it meant to love and serve God.

In our busy world of schedules, separated houses, and multiple demands, we have found it necessary to program discipleship. We find Bible studies for "Ten Basic Steps for Christian Maturity" and the "Design for Discipleship." These titles imply that after completing this series, the person will be a mature disciple. If we are able to complete ten Bible study books or if we can memorize verses, we may falsely assume that we have become disciples, without ever dealing with weightier matters of our characters, attitudes, or relationships to others. While these study tools can help us mature as disciples, they are not complete in themselves.

Discipleship programs must involve "real-life" Christianity rather than book learning alone. Discipleship is a life-growth process. The example of the leaders and the relationships between students and leaders are the best tools for discipleship.

Having offered all of these disclaimers about discipleship programs, however, let me say that I believe in them. They help both students and leaders grow in their knowledge of God's Word, and they help develop relationships that can result in the account-ability and support needed for consistent growth.

Requirements for Good Discipleship in Youth Ministry

A discipleship program must include a balance between training and the less tangible factors like interpersonal relationships, leaders' examples, and accountability. In an effort to foster discipleship in our youth ministry, we have identified six foundations for growth.

1. *Leaders' attitudes.* First, leaders need an attitude of expectancy. The leader who thinks, "Yes! It can be done!" when contemplating a challenge to teenagers will go much further than the pessimist who doubts that adolescents can grow in their faith.

Second, leaders need adaptability to the needs of young people. To assume that discipleship looks the same at every phase of life is fallacious. For a thirty-two year old, discipleship may mean getting God's perspective on achievements, possessions, or desires for success. For a teenager, the issues are likely to be peer pressure, sexual morality, or questions about marriage. Effective discipleship with teenagers involves focus on their concerns rather than our own so that our discipleship efforts address their real-life concerns.

Third, leaders need patience. Enduring the questions of the talkative student and probing the quiet student is all part of discipleship with young people. We need patience to wait through the times when we see no evidence of growth in the students' lives.

Dave, one of our discipleship leaders, focused his attention on Kirk, a quiet ninth grader. For four years, Dave worked with Kirk; he was expectant, adaptable, and patient. But Dave still wondered if he had had any effect. It wasn't until Kirk graduated from college that Dave heard about the effect that he had had. In a letter to Dave, Kirk said that Dave had been the most important Christian influence in his life, his mentor. Dave had been a good discipler, but it took him eight years to find out how good.

2. *Relationships.* Effective discipleship programming should recognize that relationships are the most important training tool in the discipleship process. The Holy Spirit works not only through Scripture and prayer but also through human relationships.

Choosing the right combination of leaders and students is essential. When planning these combinations, consider three critical factors: gender, age, and the spiritual maturity of the leader.

We have found that the most effective combinations are males with males and females with females. Coed discipleship groups can diminish honesty and can accelerate the desire to impress someone else. An older male discipling a younger female or an older female discipling a younger male is an invitation for romance or rumors— neither of which help the disciple-making process.

Our experience leads us to keep the age groups together. To think that ninth graders and twelfth graders can be combined effectively is to ignore the dramatic changes in world view and maturity that take place during those four years.

The spiritual maturity of the leaders is also important. We use the motto, "You can take a student only as far as you have been yourself." This motto not only indicates the need for staff leaders to be growing, but it also suggests that immature staff leaders will produce immature disciples. Effective discipleship programs pair less mature staff as co-leaders with more mature staff so that both students and volunteer leaders can grow.

3. *Faithfulness.* The example of Jesus and the story of Dave and Kirk illustrate one basic truth: *discipleship takes time.* Since we are dealing with character development and the long-term process of growth, we can't expect hasty results or immediate returns on our investments.

Discipleship is like the smoothing of granite rocks in New England mountain streams. When a piece of granite falls from the mountain into the rushing stream, the rock is jagged, rough, and sharp. The rock doesn't change much in a week or a month, but over the course of years, the pounding waters wear down the rough rock so it becomes as smooth as glass. The same is true of discipleship: the effects of the Bible study, prayer, and relationships can't be seen in a few weeks or months, but over a longer period of time, growth becomes noticeable, the rough spots begin to be made smooth.

The most effective discipleship groups continue through long periods of time. Donna started working with Jennifer in high school and maintained their discipleship/support group for four years. Over the course of time, Jennifer grew dramatically because of Donna's continued investment. In contrast, failure usually occurs as the result of sporadic or irregular investment. If leaders commit themselves to students but then cancel meetings and fail to prepare adequately, students not only will become disillusioned, they may give up on their faith.

4. *Accountability.* Holding each other accountable is never easy, because no one likes to be confronted with his or her failures or weaknesses. Accountability, however, is needed for consistent growth. "Better is open rebuke than hidden love. Wounds from a friend can be trusted" (Prov. 27:5–6a). Open rebukes and "wounds" to those we love are all part of the growth process.

Gary was in a discipleship group because his mother thought it would be good for him. He hated it. He never prepared, never participated, and often undermined serious discussions with mocking remarks. When the group began to deteriorate, the leader gave Gary an ultimatum—either join in or leave. Gary loved controversy, so he went home and told his mother that the group leader was kicking him out of the group. After several meetings with Gary, his mother, and an elder, the leader finally asked Gary to leave the group.

The best way to foster the growth that comes from accountability is to get commitments established before the group begins its program. Some groups sign covenants that establish the guidelines for the group. Other groups also encourage parents to sign a form that says, in effect, "I will do my best to encourage my child to fulfill the growth responsibilities related to this discipleship group."

Students and parents should understand that the group will emphasize growth in Christian disciplines (like daily quiet time) and will hold members accountable for the completion of assignments (like memorization or Bible study). Group leaders also may want to send a letter to parents encouraging them not to *force* their teenagers to join a discipleship group unless the students are willing to make a deep personal commitment to the group.

5. *Organized learning.* Although discipleship Bible studies will not produce disciples, they are effective tools in the discipleship

process. Required Bible study, organized Scripture memorization, and regulated experiences in witnessing are all part of the discipleship process. Organizing these components into an effective process is essential to success.

At one church, discipleship leaders design their own curricula and lesson plans, which are checked by the youth leader for balance in areas like Bible study, doctrinal learning, and prayer. Then the leaders spend a year of intense, specialized work with small groups of committed young men and women. Several leaders have had the same discipleship group for three or more years. In this context, discipleship is focused and highly effective.

For most youth groups, however, the situation is not so ideal. Leaders don't have time to write a year's worth of curriculum material, and students may not be ready to make an intense commitment. In this situation, the youth leader must draw on the resources of others for the organized agenda of learning within the discipleship program.

6. *Coordination within the whole program.* Discipleship programs shouldn't conflict with other youth activities or be an appendage to the youth program. Instead, we need to leave time in the overall program so that leaders and students don't get burned out by the time commitment.

One way to incorporate the discipleship time into the normal program is to have the discipleship groups meet together for dinner and for study a few hours before the normal midweek meeting. This arrangement has several advantages: it allows for the informality that can help students share more freely; it requires only one night out for students and staff; it requires only one night of transportation for parents; and if planned properly, it also can get student leaders motivated for a larger group outreach (later that same evening—at which time they can be actively reaching out to new students). However, this arrangement also has disadvantages: it separates the discipleship group students from the rest of the group and it can allow a false sense of spirituality to develop.

Discipleship Works!

Our most successful discipleship program occurred several years ago. Several staff members had discipling experience and were eager to work with our youth. We modified the Navigators' *2:7 Series* (cutting the work load in half so that students weren't overwhelmed by the homework assignments each week). We fit the program into the overall youth plan, and students in discipleship groups were given opportunities to lead, give testimonies, or witness within the youth program, thus putting into practice what they were learning in their groups. That year, over half of our students went through discipleship groups and provided the foundation for one of our best ministry years ever.

The numerical results were exciting, but even more exciting is the ongoing growth of the students who went through these groups. Some are now youth leaders, Christian leaders on their college campuses, or spiritual leaders in their communities. They have been living testimonies of the principle outlined in 2 Timothy 2:2—growing as a Christian and then passing on to others what you have learned.

Whether in large results or small, discipleship with teenagers can be the most rewarding aspect of youth ministry. Through the life changes related to discipleship groups, we can experience the great joy of seeing our lives bear "fruit that will last" (John 15:16) in the lives of others.

The great discipling year I cited above is not the reason that I believe discipling works in the youth ministry, however. Craig is the reason that I believe discipleship works. Craig was in my first discipleship group. We plodded through the book of Romans that summer, and although I tried to maintain my optimism, I really thought the summer was a waste. The six guys came together every week, but the study of Romans seemed totally boring. The only time the group perked up was when they talked about the Three Stooges or got ready for refreshments. I thought they were enduring the summer Bible study so that they could get to the refreshments.

In spite of few apparent results, I wanted to keep encouraging Craig. We corresponded while I was at college and met together when I returned. Since that time, I have watched his progress through college and have enjoyed his faithful service for five years on our junior high staff. He has led six of our youth mission teams, and he became the champion of the discipling ministry in the junior high group.

To this day, Craig mentions that Bible study when we get together. It reminds me to be patient and to be faithful to the discipling vision. Craig has been a faithful man who has affected the lives of many others, and—by his own admission—the discipleship group helped him to get started. Craig is the reason I believe that youth discipling works.

20.
ORGANIZING FOR STUDENT LEADERSHIP

Tom Skinner tells the humorous story of a zealous college student who went early to class each day and wrote on the blackboard, "Christ is the Answer!" After about a week of prophetic announcements like this, a response appeared on the same board: "What's the question?"

Is this the way we are as leaders? Are we answering the questions before they are asked, or are we giving answers to questions our students are not really asking? The issue of relevance is very tenuous in youth ministry. We simultaneously have to be giving the answers to students' genuine needs (which they may not even be aware of) while we are gaining credibility with them by answering their felt needs from a Christian viewpoint.

One of the ways to make sure we are staying relevant is to involve students as leaders. In a sense, we are missionaries to the youth culture, and we must address the gospel to that culture. Effective transmission of the gospel, however, doesn't just mean that we are constantly leading and talking and staying in charge. If the youth "church" is to grow, we need to raise up indigenous leadership. Like missionaries, it may at times be easier to keep the leadership all to ourselves (after all, it can keep us from heresies, embarrassing decisions, and blunders in leadership), but it is far better for our disciples if we learn to let them lead according to their gifts and abilities.

Leadership Styles

Many youth experts see three basic leadership styles. The first style is *staff run, staff led*. In this case, the adult leaders (the staff) lead the ministry through their experience and ideas; the leaders rely on youth resources and even feedback from students, but they make the basic program decisions. The adult leaders run the ministry: they do the directing and students are passive observers.

The second leadership style is *staff led, student run*. In this case, the leaders make the basic decisions about what the youth program should entail, but the students run the ministry. They lead singing, do some teaching, and genuinely own the program.

The third style is *student led, student run*. In this case, the students design the program and take responsibility for running it. Although this style is valid, we won't give it serious consideration here. With students running the ministry, the discipleship and leadership functions in the youth group are greatly reduced; age, lack of experience, and naïveté about life make it difficult for them to disciple each other effectively. This leadership style usually occurs only in youth ministries where students have no sponsors or adult leaders.

The advantage of the first style—staff led, staff run—is that it gives the leaders much control. They can regulate the program, insure the responsible outcome of program details, and take away the unknowns or variables that can come from students in leadership. In addition, the first style allows for training staff members in leadership skills. The disadvantage of the first style is that the students are reduced to passive spectators. They don't learn leadership skills and as a result, they aren't equipped to move into leadership positions after they leave the youth ministry. If they sit as spectators for the four or six years of their youth ministry experience, they are taught that ministry leadership is reserved for the professionals and is not the responsibility of every member of the body of Christ.

The second style—staff led, student run—offers the most advantages. Although the leaders are responsible for the direction and programming of the youth group, students are allowed to contribute their ideas as well as their growing leadership skills.

This option makes use of staff experience, maturity, and wisdom, but it allows students to test their leadership abilities with the staff alongside to help them gain confidence, to refine their rough points, and to offer correction when needed. The "staff led, student run" ministry also allows for stability in the youth ministry. Adults, especially those who stay with the ministry over a longer period, are capable of seeing the long-term implications of decisions and are able to direct the youth ministry away from some of the unproductive programs that students might choose for themselves.

Involving Students as Leaders

Assuming that the staff—with some student feedback and input, of course—plan the basic direction of the youth ministry, how can students be used as leaders? First, they can be used as leaders only when the adults are willing to delegate. If we as leaders try to keep all of the responsibilities to ourselves, we may grow, but our students' growth will be stunted.

If students are given leadership responsibilities, we must be willing to work with them to help them succeed. Good delegation means *good instruction* (telling the students what the job is that needs to be done), *good encouragement* (cheering them along in the process), and *good follow-through* (affirming and correcting them after the task is completed).

What responsibilities can involve students in the ministry?

1. *Physical responsibilities.* Students can handle responsibilities like:

- setting up the chairs for the meeting
- passing out songbooks or Bibles
- bringing or serving refreshments
- running the film projector
- handling the registration for the retreat or program
- taking attendance at Sunday school

Obviously, the physical responsibilities are not glamourous, but they are a place to start and can help students find a place in the youth group. I remember Lee, a tenth grader, who didn't fit in well with other students but his ability to run audio-visual equipment made him a very important person in the youth group. I'm convinced that he came to youth events just because he felt needed (and we looked for uses of audio-visual equipment so that he would come!).

Two years ago, we decided to start a record and tape-lending library in our youth ministry. For about four months, one of our lay leaders ran the library, and it achieved minimum success. Then Dan, an eleventh grader, took it over. Working with a staff person's assistance, he designed library cards, organized the library, and promoted the tapes and albums with much greater success (because students listened when he said that an album was "awesome"). Dan grew in his own confidence as a leader/organizer because of the basic physical responsibility of running that record and tape library.

2. *Program responsibilities.* Program responsibilities may involve song leading, participation in skits, or doing the youth group announcements. Program responsibilities need not be spiritually connected, so these jobs can be opened up to those who are not the spiritual pacesetters.

In an attempt to involve more students in weekly youth group activities, we designed a program that involved each age group (ninth grade through twelfth grade) in leading the youth program for one night each month. The seniors led first because they had the most experience and ideas; the freshmen led last.

During those months, several things happened. Students who never came to activities started attending because they were involved. Class groupings developed a sense of "team unity." There was a greater enthusiasm in the youth group because each age group tried to outdo the others. We found that students who didn't like programs with adults in front doing all the leading would come when they found themselves in charge. Giving them program responsibilities helped them to feel a greater sense of ownership.

3. *People responsibilities.* Students also can be given leadership responsibilities for the care of people. These responsibilities require

some spiritual maturity, but students can effectively do them if the adult leaders are willing to offer the instruction, encouragement, and feedback needed.

Some people responsibilities that students can undertake include

a. welcoming newcomers—both at the meeting and with a follow-up phone call or visit

b. recruiting students for retreats, Sunday school, or youth activities

c. caring for other students (We designed a "carers" program in which each student leader was responsible to care for four other students. The "carer" would call these four students if they missed a youth group function; send them cards at special times; such as birthdays or Christmas and pray for them regularly. The program gave some excellent pastoral experience to the students who took their responsibilities seriously.).

d. counseling or evangelizing other students (Through the *Youth Evangelism Explosion* program, we have been able to use many students as peer counselors. On one retreat, a first-time counselor, Kristy, was able to pray with Linda to receive Christ; Linda understood the gospel better because it was presented by a peer, and Kristy was ecstatic to see God use her life to affect someone else for Christ.)

4. *Spiritual responsibilities.* The Scriptures warn against putting a young Christian into a position of spiritual responsibility too soon. Paul wrote to Timothy (1 Tim. 3:6) that the hasty exaltation of a young Christian to leadership could result in conceit (the Greek word is related to the term for smoke and implies that a young convert's self-image can become "clouded" by the prestige). This warning should cause us to save the spiritual responsibilities for those who are the most mature in our groups. It also should remind us of the need to support student leaders through a solid discipleship program that will provide the accountability and teaching they need not only to undertake spiritual responsibilities but also to keep them from pride.

Spiritual responsibilities that students can handle with the assistance and supervision of a discipling staff person include

a. teaching a Sunday school class or leading a small group

b. discipling peers (Usually older students working with younger ones of the same sex works best.)

c. motivating others to rise to spiritual challenges (Many of our student missionaries go on missions because of the challenges they hear from their peers who have gone on trips before.)

d. writing tracts or other material to reach their peers

Julie was given spiritual responsibility in eighth grade as the junior high prayer coordinator. Through her efforts, the whole junior high ministry became more aware of and committed to the power of prayer. For Melanie, spiritual responsibility meant the assumption of leadership on her mission team. In spite of the fact that she was only a high school junior, her spiritual depth qualified her to lead when both adult female leaders got sick.

Problems with Student Leadership

Putting students in charge of aspects of the ministry may help them feel a greater sense of ownership and participation, but it also opens the adult leaders to more problems. Citing these problems shouldn't discourage us from developing student leaders, but it can prevent the surprises when a few things go wrong.

1. *Pride.* Paul was right in his caution to Timothy about young leaders. The feeling of superiority or haughtiness can overtake a young person who repeatedly stands in front of the group, gets the applause, or even sees God at work through him or her. In the teenage world, where popularity is so important, too much leadership responsibility can cause a student to become "puffed up." It also can separate that student from his or her peers because of the aloofness that the student might project. To avoid this problem, make sure the student is in a discipleship relationship where his or her pride can be checked.

2. *Irresponsibility.* I have set up the chairs myself. I have dashed to the variety store to buy refreshments when the student in charge of refreshments did not show up. Students (like adults) will fail. They will make us feel that delegating is more difficult than doing it ourselves—and sometimes it is! To avoid this problem, stay in touch with students to remind them of their responsibilities.

And when they fail, don't say, "Oh, it was nothing." Forgive them, but don't diminish the significance of an unfulfilled responsibility.

3. *Parents.* Giving students responsibility may sound great to us, but the parents may not be so enthusiastic. To avoid this problem, communicate with both parents and students so that everyone knows what is expected.

4. *Failure.* Allowing students to lead doesn't guarantee their success. I was elated when John signed up to participate in the talent show on one of our retreats. I thought to myself, "At last he is coming out of his shell." On Saturday night, John did his performance and made a *total* fool of himself. Students laughed *at* him—not *with* him. The guy was devastated. John took some responsibilities, but he blew it. To avoid this problem, make sure an adult leader is available to encourage and support the student if he or she fails.

5. *Limited experience.* It is frustrating to plan with a group of students, only to have them draw a complete blank when we say, "Well, what do *you* think we should do? You're the leader!" Because their experience is limited to their few teenage years, they will rely on us for ideas. To avoid this problem, direct students to outside resources that can generate ideas for them. *Group* magazine, the *Ideas* library, or the *Any Old Time* series are all potential resources for student planning.

6. *Disillusionment.* The title of David Elkind's *All Grown Up and No Place To Go* reminds us to let teenagers enjoy the teen years. We don't need to produce what he calls "adultified children" who are old and mature before their time. We must be cautious not to push teenagers to be leaders too fast, for this can cause them to lose their motivation to grow up.

Von Trutzschler, one of the nation's true youth ministry veterans, shares this sad account of the disillusionment in students who were pushed to leadership too fast:

> I used to work hard with my junior highs, giving them leadership responsibilities in meetings and platform exposure. There were kids in the group who could handle programs and speak. I could walk out of the room, leaving no adults present, and come back an hour later to a controlled meeting, going on exactly as planned in our elections. We

had a board of leading youth directors and pastors who checked out those that wanted to run for office, gave special awards to outgoing officers, and recognition for those who stood out. All this was on the junior high level. But I lost many of those individuals when they became 11th and 12th graders, and I was disappointed because I had put so much time into them. They were doing so well when suddenly they would peel off and go into the world. I encountered some of them later, and these were their comments: "We had enough of this Mickey Mouse stuff. We wanted to go into the world where it's real. We wanted to have some fun. We wanted to live." That hit me hard. In growing more mature, many of my best potential leaders threw off their junior high lifestyle, and along with it went their intense involvement in the youth program. So I changed my philosophy. Many of us have been pushing too soon and too fast, trying to develop what we see as leadership. Kids are good mimics (in the platform sense), but they often lack the maturity, judgment, and wisdom it takes to be real leaders.[1]

To avoid this problem, try to give students responsibility to match their age and maturity. Let students be "kids" in their teen years, especially in the early teens.

7. *Limitations.* In addition to experience and maturity, students may also be limited in the time they can offer. Students with leadership potential often are recruited for many leadership responsibilities—from football captain to band leader to Latin Club president. To avoid this problem, delegate responsibilities that can be handled within the context of the student's other time commitments.

8. *Spiritual inconsistency.* I don't mind letting a student who is uncommitted to Christ set up the chairs, but I refuse to let students lead meetings if their lives contradict the Scriptures. I once had to "fire" a student leader because his behavior with his girlfriend in public was so physical that his status as a spiritual leader was discredited. To avoid this problem, help students understand that leadership means a higher standard of personal responsibility.

Five Steps Toward Better Leadership

If students are to develop to their fullest potential as leaders, we must be willing to take five basic steps to assist them in the process:

---

[1] "Youth Ministry Is More Than a Meeting," in *The Youth Leader's Sourcebook,* Gary Dausey, ed. (Grand Rapids, MI: Zondervan, 1983), 46–47.

1. *Hear them out.* Surveys, forum discussions, and other feedback times will help us learn about students' needs and where they can be stretched and challenged.

2. *Use them.* We need to give them responsibilities that they can handle so that they come to *their* group, not *our* group.

3. *Affirm them.* Students are much more likely to keep on taking responsibility (and to rebound from failures) when they know our affirmation and encouragement. We must be careful not to take our student leaders for granted.

4. *Let them testify.* The best way to recruit more student leaders is to let those who have served as leaders tell others about how they have grown through the experience of leadership.

5. *Be a facilitator.* When students start to lead on their own, our jobs will change from omnipresent leader to facilitator. When students start their own small groups or host their own socials, we may no longer be needed at these meetings. Our students will need only our advice about how to lead. When we come to this point, we can rejoice, for we will know that they own the program.

Resources For Part III

YOUTH MINISTRY AND YOUTH PROGRAMMING

Ameiss, Bill. *Getting It Together in Youth Ministry*. Wheaton, Illinois: Ministries Unlimited, n.d.

Benson, Dennis C., and Wolfe, Bill. *The Basic Encyclopedia for Youth Ministry*. Loveland, Colorado: Group Books, 1981.

Benson & Senter (eds.). *Complete Book of Youth Ministry*. Chicago: Moody Press, 1987.

Burns, Jim, and Yaconelli, Mike. *High School Ministry*. Grand Rapids: Zondervan Publishing House, 1986.

Campolo, Anthony. *Ideas for Social Action*. El Cajon, California: Youth Specialties, 1983.

Clapp, Steve, and Cook, Jerry O. *Youth Worker's Handbook*. Sidell, Illinois: C-4 Resources, 1981.

Coleman, James S., *et. al. Youth: Transition to Adulthood*. Chicago: University of Chicago Press, 1974.

Dausey, Gary (ed.). *The Youth Leader's Sourcebook*. Grand Rapids: Zondervan Publishing House, 1983.

Ludwig, Glenn. *Building an Effective Youth Ministry*. Nashville, Tennessee: Abingdon Press, 1979.

Lynn, David. *The Youth Group Planning Calendar*. El Cajon, California: Youth Specialties, 1985.

Richards, Lawrence O. *Youth Ministry: Its Renewal in the Local Church*. Grand Rapids: Zondervan Publishing House, 1987.

Roadcup, David (ed.). *Ministering to Youth: A Handbook for the Eighties*. Cincinnati, Ohio: Standard Publishing, 1980.

Schultz, Joani (ed.). *Youth Ministry Cargo*. Loveland, Colorado: Group Books, 1986.

Stevens, Doug. *Called To Care*. Grand Rapids: Zondervan Publishing House, 1985.

Teeter, Ruth, *et. al.* (eds.). *Youthwork Bibliography*. St. Paul, Minnesota: Center for Youth Development and Research, 1980.

Willey, Ray (ed.). *Working With Youth: A Handbook for the Eighties*. Wheaton, Illinois: Victor Books, 1982.

Zuck, Roy, and Benson, Warren (eds.). *Youth Education in the Church*. Chicago: Moody Press, 1978.

YOUTH AND MISSIONS
Bolinder, Garth, McKee, Tom and Cionca, John R. *Music, Youth and Education*. Carol Stream, Illinois: CTI Publications, 1986.

YOUTH AND EVANGELISM
Coleman, Robert E. *The Master Plan of Evangelism*. Old Tappan, New Jersey: Fleming H. Revell, 1964.

Eims, Leroy. *Winning Ways*. Wheaton, Illinois: Scripture Press, 1974.

Hartley, Fred. *Dare To Be Different*. Old Tappan, New Jersey: Fleming H. Revell, 1980.

Innes, Dick. *I Hate Witnessing*. Ventura, California: Vision House, 1983.

Keefauver, Larry. *Friends and Faith*. Loveland, Colorado: Group Books, 1986.

Little, Paul E. and others. *HIS Guide to Evangelism*. Downers Grove, Illinois: InterVarsity Press, 1977.

Little, Paul E. *How To Give Away Your Faith*. Downers Grove, Illinois: InterVarsity Press, 1966.

Manley-Pippert, Rebecca. *Out of the Salt-Shaker and Into the World*. Downers Grove, Illinois: InterVarsity Press, 1979.

Stewart, Ed. *Outreach to Youth*. Glendale, California: Gospel Light Publications, 1978.

JUNIOR HIGH MINISTRY
Holderness, Ginny. *The Exuberant Years*. Atlanta, Georgia: John Knox, 1971.

Junior High Ministry magazine published by *Group* magazine, P.O. Box 481, Loveland, Colorado.

Rice, Wayne. *Junior High Ministry Revised Edition*. Grand Rapids: Zondervan Publishing House, 1987.

Shaheen, David. *Growing a Junior High Ministry*. Loveland, Co.: Group Books 1986.

Stafford, Linda, and Burns, Ridge. *How To Plan and Direct Junior High Super Stars*. Wheaton, Illinois: Victor Books, 1983.

PROGRAM AIDS
Any Old Time series. Wheaton, Illinois: Victor Books.
Campus Life magazine. Carol Stream, Illinois.

Group magazine. Loveland, Colorado.

Holck, Manfred, Jr. *Annual Budgeting*. Minneapolis, Minnesota: Augsburg Publishing House, 1977.

The Idea Library. Published by Youth Specialties (El Cajon, California).

Lynn, David and Mike Yaconelli. *Tension Getters*. Grand Rapids: Zondervan Publishing House, 1981.

_____. *Tension Getters II*. Grand Rapids: Zondervan Publishing House, 1985.

Rice, Wayne, and Mike Yaconelli. *Creative Socials*. Grand Rapids: Zondervan Publishing House, 1986.

_____. *Holiday Ideas*. Grand Rapids: Zondervan Publishing House, 1981.

_____. *Play It!* Grand Rapids: Zondervan Publishing House, 1986.

Rice, Wayne. *Great Ideas for Small Youth Groups*. Grand Rapids: Zondervan Publishing House, 1986.

Youthworker Journal. Published quarterly by Youth Specialties (El Cajon, California).

CURRICULUM RESOURCES

Burns, Jim. *Putting God First*. Eugene, Oregon: Harvest House, 1982.

Campus Crusade for Christ. *The Ten Basic Steps*. San Bernadino, California: Here's Life Publishers, 1968.

McAllister, Dawson. *Manual for Student Relationships* (three volumes). Dallas, Texas: Roper Press, 1975.

_____. *Manual for Student Discipleship*, (two volumes). Chicago: Moody Press, 1978.

_____. *A Walk With Christ to the Cross*. Englewood, Colorado: Shepherd Productions, 1980.

_____. *A Walk With Christ Through the Resurrection*. Englewood, Colorado: Shepherd Productions, 1981.

The Navigators. *2:7 Series*, (6 volumes), 1978. *The Topical Memory System*. Colorado Springs, Colorado: Navigator Press, 1973.

_____. *The Design for Discipleship Series*, (7 volumes). Colorado Springs, Colorado: Navigator Press, 1973.

St. Clair, Barry. *Leadership*. Wheaton, Illinois: Victor Books, 1985.

von Trutzschler, E.G. and Rick Bundschuh. *Dicipleship I*. Ventura, California: Gospel Light, 1984.

Part IV

EVALUATION

"By this," Jesus said, "all men know that you are my disciples." The standards of love, obedience, and worship are incorporated into our Lord's words to his disciples. Perhaps he offered these words as a summary of his other teaching, but his phrascology, "By this all men know," also points us to the need for evaluation. In effect, Jesus was telling his disciples and us: "Here are the standards by which you should measure yourselves; when you match yourselves against these, you will *know* how you are doing."

If only we could evaluate our youth ministries with simple, objective tools. If only we could work through a checklist and say, "There. The work is done; it is as good as it will ever be."

But we can't. Youth ministry—because it is people ministry—is never quite done. There is always time to make one more phone call, talk with one more student, or study just five minutes more. Youth ministry can always grow and improve. Indeed, the self-satisfied complacency that says, "It's as good as it will ever be," often leads to spiritual pride (1 Cor. 10:12).

So how do we evaluate? If our personal lives and our ministry goals are to be kept in balance, we can't measure ourselves against a standard that says, "Everything is done," for we'll fail every time.

Instead, we can take a step back, ask ourselves where we are, and look for ways that we need to grow.

We should submit ourselves not only to self-examination but also to evaluation from others. The people around us often can provide the valuable objectivity we need.

The evaluation questions in chapter 21 will help us see our youth ministry flaws that we perhaps can correct. The spiritual advice of chapter 22 will remind us of the ultimate purposes of the youth ministry—spiritual growth. And as you evaluate and reflect, remember that God is sovereign. He can take even our failures and use them for good. In that confidence, we can evaluate without fear.

I was reminded of this one summer as we flew home from Zambia on our most zealous mission trip ever. A team of fifteen had worked for three weeks to get electric wiring across a mile and a half stretch of open plain from a hospital generator to a Bible school. The trip had involved much traveling, a myriad of details, and eighteen months of planning. Now it was over, and I was meeting with students to do individual evaluation.

When I asked Holly, Steve, Jeff, and Debbie to compare this trip to other missions they had served on, they all said the same thing. They loved the Zambia trip, but they had learned more on a previous trip to West Germany. Why? "Because more things went wrong there." All four answered the same way.

They explained that lost baggage, administrative oversights, errant train connections, and an injured team member had been used by God to force that team to depend more on each other and on God. Our Zambia mission had gone more smoothly, but they had learned more from an experience that I had considered an administrative nightmare. My evaluation was not the same as God's: I could only see the failures; he used the failures and problems to change lives.

This is the perspective that we must keep as we start to evaluate. It is God who is at work through all our efforts— successes and failures—to do his good work, both in the process of changing us and in the process of helping our youth group members, co-leaders, and parents to grow.

The writer of Proverbs observed that "a righteous man falls seven times [over and over] and rises again" (Prov. 24:16). The righteous person is not one who never falls; indeed, he or she may fall repeatedly. Rather, the righteous person is the one who *when* he or she falls, gets up, accepts God's forgiveness, and starts afresh.

Evaluating our ministries and the spiritual growth that occurs within these ministries may knock us down by showing us where we have failed, but these "knock downs" are for our growth. With this in mind, let's see how we are doing.

21.
MEASURING EFFECTIVENESS IN YOUTH MINISTRY

I envy students. Every few months they get a report card that evaluates their growth. They are told how they are doing, where they need to improve, and how they can be sure they will graduate to the next level of their "career."

Ministry, however, doesn't have such a reporting system. We get no report cards that tell us when we are doing well or warning cards when we are failing. Measuring our effectiveness is an elusive task.

How can we tell if the youth ministry is going well? Are numbers the best gauge? Do unique programs guarantee that we are doing our best? Does a meaningful retreat measure our ministry's success?

People measure the effectiveness of youth ministry in many ways. Some point to the number of unchurched students we have reached. Others point to relevance or big groups or flashy programs. How do we measure?

Evaluating our youth ministry requires that we know who is asking the questions, what the questions are, and what we should do with the answers.

IDENTIFY THE JUDGES

Who evaluates the youth group? Ultimately, God himself is our judge. He declares us forgiven or effective or healthy by the standards of Scripture. He reassures us that our youth ministry is important, even when outside circumstances may tempt us to think otherwise. In the midst of apparent failures, he can let us know his grace and peace.

The opinion of the judge, however, is general. God's Word can tell us how to live or the qualities that should characterize our groups; personal time with God can shape our leadership qualities, standards of behavior, or relational effectiveness, but it may not give us an overall sense of the quality of a retreat, the long-term growth in a junior high student, or the way to deal with a troubled family.

To assist us in the evaluation process, we must incorporate others as judges. Who sits with us to measure our youth ministry's effectiveness? Who is the "jury"?

1. *Partners in ministry.* Spouses, fellow pastors, or volunteers who work with us often have the most realistic view of our youth ministry and of our effectiveness as leaders. They can sit back and evaluate without the subjective involvement that we might have. My wife keeps me from becoming overly optimistic or pessimistic. My peers help me look sanely at how I am doing as a leader.

Partners in the ministry can help us identify strengths and weaknesses that we might otherwise overlook. They can offer constructive criticism, point us to resources, or affirm us when we are discouraged. "Wounds from a friend can be trusted," Proverbs tells us; our friends can wound us for the sake of our own growth and the sake of the ministry.

My partner in ministry, Tim, has served as a very valuable critic in our youth ministry. After over ten years of ministry in the same place, I was getting dull, and Tim came with some healthy and challenging questions. "Do you realize that there is very little Bible *study* going on?" "How long since you've talked on sex and dating?" "Shouldn't we start using the video resources available for teaching?"

Without such questions, I'm sure my dullness would have increased, but our ministry has grown because of these healthy questions.

2. *The young people.* Other youth leaders often ask, "How can I tell if my program (or Bible study or Sunday school) is effective

with my teenagers?" Many are quite surprised when I respond, "Why don't you ask your students?"

Our teenagers are great resources and sources of feedback because they are right in the center of the teen world. They know what reaches them and what doesn't. Questions like, "Are you feeling at home with our group?" or "Do these lessons help you understand and apply the Bible to everyday life?" will help us determine whether or not we are reaching our students.

Beware, though, because teenagers are not subtle. "Did you enjoy the retreat?" I asked one student (secretly hoping that he would comment on the quality of my talks). "Oh yeah," he exclaimed, "the girls in your youth group are *awesome*." Oh, well. . . .

3. *The parents.* For many youth leaders, the parents are viewed more like the executioners after the trial rather than the objective jurors. Nevertheless, we can't evaluate our effectiveness without consulting them. Parents can give us good insight into what makes their teenagers tick, what programs are working well, or how consistently our students are applying the gospel to daily living.

A parent advisory board in the earliest days of my youth ministry was very helpful to me. A group of ten parents met with me monthly to talk about programs, to discuss ways that our youth group was succeeding and failing, and to brainstorm with me. At first the advisory board made me feel scared, defensive, or judged, but I eventually learned that these parents wanted the youth group to succeed even more than I did. Through them, I could learn what students talked about on the phone, what the "hot" movies or TV shows were, and what student responses were to youth group Bible studies.

4. *Church leaders.* The elders, deacons, or other ruling body in the church can inspire fear in any youth worker. To see the chairman of the board headed my way on a Sunday morning after an outreach concert still makes my knees tremble, but we need to hear from these leaders so that we can understand where the youth group fits into the priorities of the church at large.

Talking with church leaders helps us see if we are meeting church or ministry expectations of the youth group. I know of one leader who was reaching a large number of street kids, and he easily could have settled back and thought, "Wow, things are really going great." He was devastated, however, to learn that—in his church's opinion—he was missing the mark. The church leaders' priority was a ministry to children of church families. This youth leader resolved the question of expectations by giving himself to the church youth and training them to reach the street kids, but he could have saved himself a lot of grief by identifying the church's expectations in the first place.

5. *Outside observers.* Youth leaders from other ministries or other people in our own churches can be the most objective observers and evaluators. Allowing them to look over our program, watch us in action, or talk about our priorities can help reveal our own ministerial astigmatisms.

I was humiliated one day as I was having lunch with a fellow youth worker. I shared my frustrations about unappreciative kids, griping parents, and failed programs. As the older man sitting in the next booth stood to leave, he turned to me and said, "Let me ask you one question: do you *love* the teens you are working with?" Then he left. What a slap in the face! But I needed the rebuke, and this unknown exhorter helped me see that a good portion of my problems was in my own lack of love, not in my students or their parents.

ASK THE HARD QUESTIONS

No one likes to squirm under the pressure of questions like "Do you *love* your kids?" But we must face those questions if we are to grow. In our ministry, we evaluate by asking these seven questions:

1. *Are students' needs being met?* Youth ministry needs to be addressed to the felt needs (like what does a Christian do about rock music?) as well as the real needs (like understanding the truth that Jesus is God) of young people. We must look at our ministry's ability to address both as one way to measure our effectiveness.

How relevant is our ministry? Are we answering questions that no one is asking? Are we talking to our junior high students about when it is permissible to kiss when they are wondering about saving their virginity? Are we having seminars on career planning when our students are scarcely thinking about the next day?

We can't blame the teenagers for disinterest if the focus of the youth group is irrelevant to their worlds and needs. We must listen to them, get to know the pressures that they face, and come into their worlds if we are to be effective.

2. *Are our students learning the basics of faith?* We must not spend all our time on the felt needs alone. If students know all of the answers about sexual morality, but they are unable to articulate the message of salvation, we will produce moral, nice people, but they will be incapable of leading others to faith.

Jacques Ellul has written, "We must not shelter the young from the world's dangers, but arm them so that they will be able to overcome them."[1] Arming our youth means not only training them in Christian responses to secular media or teen phenomena like "Dungeons and Dragons," but also equipping them in the basics of prayer, Bible study, and Christian disciplines. Certainly we need to make the learning of these basics relevant to the youth, but they *must* be a focal point of our ministries lest we build young Christians with high morality but no Scriptural foundations for what they believe.

3. *Does our ministry challenge the whole person?* The growth of Jesus in Luke 2:52 provides an apt model for youth ministry: he grew intellectually, physically, socially, and spiritually. Unfortunately, some youth ministries focus on only one of these growth aspects rather than realizing the interrelationship—especially in the teen years. A young person may find it impossible to grow spiritually in a group where she feels like a social outcast or where he thinks that his physical appearance makes everyone hate him.

Solid youth ministries need multi-faceted growth. Do our ninth grade boys need a weekend away with male leaders that they respect so that they can learn some social skills? Does the obesity of twenty-five of our students tell me that an athletic "get-in-shape" program, offered sensitively, might meet a need? Seminars on "How to study" or workshops on "Healthy relationships at home"

---

[1] Jacques Ellul, *Money and Power*, (Downers Grove, IL: InterVarsity Press, 1984), 123.

all can be part of a ministry that tries to address the multiple needs of students.

When I wrote an article about this subject for *Christianity Today*, a woman responded by pointing out an oversight in my questions, an oversight that revealed a weakness in our own youth ministry. She suggested that I add another question to my list: Are youth being taught to *worship?* If we are devoting ourselves to the growth of the whole person, we also must address their spiritual need to learn to worship the God we want them to obey.

4. *Are we building families, not just young people?* One pastor identified his ministry as "helping parents carry out *their* ministry to youth." Parents hold the greatest God-given responsibility for their young people. An effective youth ministry must seek to minister to parents and the whole family as well as to the teenager.

Building families has meant offering seminars, writing letters, and even sending out lists of books available to parents of teenagers. Parents often respond enthusiastically to the help we can offer. If we communicate that we understand a little of their fears and frustrations, and if we are willing to offer them our listening ears, whole families benefit.

5. *Are students challenged to serve?* In an age where young people are called "self-absorbed," someone needs to be challenging these same youth to live by the biblical truth, "we find ourselves by giving ourselves away in service to others."

In an October, 1985, interview in *Christianity Today*, Taylor University President, Dr. Jay Kesler, discussed the apathy of modern youth. He pointed out that their apathy was not based on their lack of information but rather on their failure to believe that they could make any difference.

Challenging young people to serve means that we challenge them to make a difference. As Christians, young people need to be equipped to do the work of the ministry (Eph. 4:11–13). We must train our teenagers to serve—each other, the elderly, the poor, and others who are beyond their normal sphere of influence.

6. *Are our students prepared to move on?* One of the greatest challenges of long-term youth ministry is that it lets us see the five- or ten-year results of our youth ministry efforts. The long-term

view helps us to see where our youth ministries need improvement in training and preparing young people for the challenges and decisions that lie ahead.

Youth need training related to the college world or the working world into which they graduate. In the short span that we work with them, we must try to supplement the learning that takes place in their homes with biblical standards about decision making, ethics, and discernment.

Effective youth ministry means taking time—especially with high school juniors and seniors—to train teenagers in the dynamics of integrating faith into the "real world," starting their own ministries, and witnessing in ways that are understandable in a secular world.

7. *Are our students gaining a vision for reaching unbelievers?* The ideals of evangelism and world missions are often missing in youth groups. This must change because we are working with the students who will lead our youth groups, churches, and mission organizations in the future. If they develop no sense of compassion for unbelievers in the teen years, it becomes increasingly difficult to build it into their lives later.

In the years when youth are most pliable, our ministries must build compassion for those without Christ. From their locker-mates to the unreached in China, youth need to be taught (and personal example is the best teacher!) to reach out, to witness, and to pray for others to become Christians. Complacency that is fostered in adolescence will be tough to extract in the adult years.

RESPOND TO THE RESULTS

After we hear from the "jury," what do we do? How do we incorporate their evaluation into our ministry?

1. *Affirmation.* Good evaluation should lead to a sense of success—at least in a few areas. Maybe we aren't reaching the whole person, but we're starting to care for parents in a new way. Maybe only a few of our students are established in the basics, but there are a few—and they might be influencing others!

If every evaluation is negative, then we must be courageous enough to do some probing. Either God has put us in a tough setting to test our stamina and trust, or it may be time to get out of youth ministry. While I am not saying that success is the measure of effectiveness or obedience to God, total failure may be God's way of telling us that our skills and gifts are mismatched to the jobs we have been given.

In most circumstances, however, the answers will be mixed. Some questions will reveal our strengths; comments from students or parents or co-workers may help us see where we are doing well. Don't overlook these positive comments. We need affirmation in youth ministry. For our own health and sense of self-worth, we need to hear the positive answers before we proceed to correct the weaknesses.

I was reminded of this recently as we sent out another mission team. This one was full of problems. Oversights, problems with leadership, and stresses between me and the team were evident. In a moment of gloominess, I thought to myself, *Why do I do this?* My wife was God's voice of affirmation: one problem doesn't nullify the dozens of successful ventures. Sure, there were problems and areas that needed correction, but I needed to remember the positive factors before I moved out to correct the negative ones.

2. *Balance.* Do the responses show some area of weakness? Then we need to start taking steps to correct the flaws. But remember the need for balance. Too often we can overreact to a negative evaluation by swinging to the opposite extreme. If the youth group is too inwardly focused, the answer is not to destroy the small group network and force everyone into street preaching. The answer is to make slow changes within the existing system to work toward the desired end.

A few years ago we evaluated our youth ministry. Parents, volunteers, and students all agreed that we needed more adult leadership. At first I was tempted to rush out to recruit anything that breathed. My supervisors, however, helped me to keep balanced. We drew up a job description of the people we needed as youth leaders, and then we began the slow process of recruiting. A balanced approach to the needs of the group enabled us to recruit those who were gifted in youth work and committed to the teenagers rather than those who were willing but not able (which would have been the result of my hasty approach).

3. *Change.* Perhaps the most courageous act of a youth worker is to discontinue a program that has outlived its effectiveness or is no longer meeting any ministry goal. A healthy evaluation will inevitably reveal that some of our efforts are ineffective, that we aren't teaching students what they need to know, or that something needs to be added.

Before making changes, however, we must go back to the jury. Do other people agree that a certain program is ineffective? If so, then we may want to work with that program and make the needed changes.

Before making changes, we also must ask if there are people in our ministry to help accomplish the changes—especially if we are considering adding something to our programs. For several years, I have wanted a support system for our single parents, but we have never had the appropriate people to do it. Each year we decided it was better not to start the program than to start it and see it fail four months into the year because it lacked leadership.

Before making changes, we also must assess our students' commitment to God (and to each other and us). A heavy-duty discipleship Bible study is an unnecessary addition if no one in the group is a Christian, but a one-month discovery study in the Gospel of John may be appropriate.

Healthy evaluation should lead to deletions, additions, and modifications. These changes are best, however, when we have a realistic picture of the group situation in which we are working.

Conclusion

I used to work in a warehouse with a young man named John. Every night when John came to work, he would greet each person with a question: "Paul, do you like me?" "Peter, do you like me?" "Joe, do you like me?" His insecure questions never ceased, and eventually no one responded. They knew neither his question nor their answers were taken seriously.

We, on the other hand, must be willing to ask evaluative questions about ourselves and our ministries if we are to be serious about our growth. We don't need to manifest the insecurities of my friend John, constantly wondering if we are liked, but we do need to be willing to examine how we are doing and whether or not our ministries' goals are being met.

Is our youth ministry effective? Gather the jury, ask the hard questions, and build for growth!

22.
MEASURING
SPIRITUAL GROWTH

Mrs. Haynes approached me after church. I could tell she was upset about something—in this case, it turned out to be Joan, her fifteen-year-old daughter. Evidently, Joan was bored with youth group and was wondering whether she wanted to come anymore. "Do you always have to have Bible study or devotionals at youth group?" asked Mrs. Haynes. "Shouldn't you put on more fun events and socials for our youth so that they'll stay in church?"

Not long after my discussion with Mrs. Haynes, Mr. Hampton called me at the church office. "Paul, I'm concerned about David (his sixteen-year-old son). He seems to be losing interest in youth group. He says that, although you do have a devotional or Bible study almost every week, you seldom get into the 'meat' of the Word. Isn't there some way to increase the spiritual growth emphasis in the youth group?"

These two cases are typical of the tensions youth workers face in helping young people grow spiritually. Some students want more fun; others seek greater spiritual depth. Some want all-night parties; others want all-night vigils. Where is the balance?

Answering this question requires that we look first to the purpose of our youth ministries: *What exactly are our goals?* Do we want to be a fun group that attracts many on a superficial level but lacks spiritual depth? Or are we building our youth groups on the principles of A. B. Bruce's *Training of the Twelve* so that non-disciples feel unwanted? Chances are, we're looking for a little of both—a place for the uncommitted student to experience the love of Christ and a place for the committed student to grow even more.

Answering the question about balance also requires that we consider how we measure growth in teenagers. What does adolescent spirituality look like? Is it turning from rock music to Debby Boone? Or forsaking Saturday nights out for personal Bible study? How do we know when spiritual maturation is taking place?

These questions have no simple answers. We *do* want students to have fun in the youth group; we don't want them to associate Christian faith with boredom or grim seriousness. Yet there must also be a time for focusing on the spiritual commitments necessary in Christian growth.

How do we keep our kids on the road to balanced spiritual maturity? Several principles can help as we seek to maximize their spiritual potential.

1. *Understand adolescent spiritual capacities.* One of our volunteer youth workers, plagued with questions about discipling young people, went to our senior pastor. "How can I tell," she asked, "if a kid is growing spiritually or just 'growing up'?"

His response was wise: "Why can't it be *both?* One of your tasks is to help young people 'grow up' next to someone who offers a Christian perspective." Young people's spiritual growth occurs within a greater context of overall growth. If we're to be effective disciplers of young people, we must address spiritual growth as it relates to the physical, social, mental, and emotional growth that they're also experiencing.

Furthermore, teenagers are often excessively pragmatic. "Living in heavenly realities" may be beyond their present interest or capacity. I'm reminded of how a teacher of two year olds summarized his teaching goals: "I teach children that God loves them and that they shouldn't hit each other." He understood his children's growth capabilities, and so should we.

2. *Adjust expectations to the age group.* Lest our youth grow up too fast, too soon, we must accept them as they are and seek to move on from there. I don't want a fourteen-year-old boy to be like me; I want him to see the reality of Christ in *his* own life, from his fourteen-year-old perspective.

I once asked five young men to join me weekly for prayer and Bible study. I called the group "The Faithful Five" because faithfulness was the most important lesson I myself had been learning. It was not, however, the most important lesson *they* had been learning. Irregular attendance, incomplete assignments, and lack of motivation plagued the group. We disbanded after five months (and renamed the group "The Failure Five"). What happened? The group failed because I projected on to them my own spiritual position.

Others of us expect too little. Junior high students on successful mission trips to Haiti, ninth-grade discipleship groups, and high school students who have led their peers to Christ have taught me not to aim too low. If we first meet students where they are, we can challenge them to go a step further than they've ever gone before.

3. *Consider external expectations.* In youth ministry, we're working not only with our own expectations but also with the expectations of others. Of course, they may not be spiritual expectations:

"The teens are too restless during the morning service. What are you doing to keep them under control?" (The pastor)

"We have a great group of young people; please keep them happy so they don't leave the church." (The church)

"I don't really care what you do with the rest of the group as long as you pay attention to my child." (The parents)

"Are we going to have fun, or do we have to talk about God and the Bible again?" (The students)

Although we can't meet everyone's expectations, we must take them into account if we are to work toward spiritual growth. No matter how noble or biblical our goals may be, we're ignoring reality if we don't recognize that these external expectations will either spur or slow our youth group's spiritual progress.

4. *Work toward real-life discipleship.* Many of our students youth are church kids. They've been going to church since they were conceived, and they know how to regurgitate spiritual truths, verses, and even Christian values with little or no thought. They're

Christianized, covered with a veneer of doctrines and cliches that keep them from opening their hearts to God. So how can this veneer be penetrated?

Real-life Christianity is the only answer. Using resources like the *Tension Getters* books (Youth Specialties) gets kids talking about life situations in ways that show what they *really* believe. Visiting the high school campus is valuable because it forces these Christianized students to explain to their friends who we are—an explanation that may be the closest they have ever come to witnessing.

One of my favorite students, Brian, met me for lunch one day. I took him to a nearby restaurant. After we were served, I said, "Brian, let's pray." I thanked God for the food—a short prayer, to the point. When I looked up, Brian was wide-eyed. He'd never thought of praying in a restaurant. Brian realized that his Christian faith is something he's supposed to carry with him into the real world. For him, praying before a meal represented the great integration of church "stuff" with daily living.

Developing spiritual potential in young people means we don't assume they understand how profound truths work themselves out in real life. Our stories and our life examples must show them.

5. *Set a personal example.* The principle "more things are caught than taught" is inescapably true in youth ministry. Ultimately, our young people—at least the ones we sincerely pour our lives into—will become *like us*. The student will become like the teacher (Luke 6:40). How frightening! What a challenge to our own spiritual growth!

Recently I was asked to evaluate the decline in attendance of my own youth group. I could point to demographic factors, inconvenient locations, tight budgets, and busy schedules. Given enough time, I could have outlined a variety of reasons that blamed programs, facilities, or other people. But one other factor convicted me. I could see—by God's grace—that much of the problem was with me. Our group's growth was hurting from my lack of desire to reach out, to welcome newcomers, and to share Christ with non-believers. My youth group had become like me.

If we want our students to grow spiritually, we must be

pacesetters and models. If we're tying to lead them to heights that we ourselves have never attempted to reach, we will become modern-day Pharisees.

6. *Recruit the help of parents.* The impact of the adult example is nowhere more important than at home. If true spiritual growth is to be realized in our youth ministry, we must ask the parents to help us. Though non-believing parents may not be willing, most Christian parents may.

Parents can help in two ways. First, they set an example. When we're challenging kids to have daily devotional times or to witness at school, we first should meet with their parents and challenge *them* to be developing in their personal time with God and in witnessing to their peers.

Second, parents can provide support of our spiritual goals for their children. We can write out the spiritual challenges the youth group is undertaking and ask parents to encourage their kids in these efforts to grow. But we must be aware that well-meaning Christian parents may want to push their children further or faster than the young people themselves may want to go. Each case must be handled individually, but generally, forced growth yields only inner rebellion (regardless of external conformity). The best solution is to ask parents to challenge and encourage their teenagers to grow without forcing it on them.

7. *Use available resources.* Although some discipleship resources can appear to be too structured or too heavy or too glib, take time to seriously examine them. They can be useful tools to generate growth (see resource suggestions in chapter 19). Such resources can be effective when they are complemented by the positive, personal attention needed for genuine growth.

Measuring the Results

The apostle Paul wrote that he worked in order to present every person *"complete* in Christ" (Col. 1:28 NASB, italics added). But what does "complete in Christ" mean for our hyperactive seventh-grade boys or our apathetic eleventh graders? How do we measure spiritual growth?

1. *Short-term results.* We start by looking at what's happening

right now. Parental responses are often the best measures: "My Jimmy is changed. He's stopped swearing, and he's consistently helping around the house. It's a miracle." In our youth group, we say, "Christian behavior begins at home." If it does, parents will notice.

Outreach is another short-term measure. As a student matures in faith, he or she often begins to see outreach as a natural outflow of Christian faith—whether it takes the form of evangelism, visiting newcomers, service projects, or whatever. As a young person begins to understand self-denial for the sake of Christ, he or she also will begin to look beyond personal needs to the needs of others.

Spiritual "markers" are another short-term measure. Dr. David Elkind speaks of the need for markers in adolescent growth to help a young person chart a course into adulthood. The same type of charting can assist a young person to grow spiritually. Although we should avoid checklist discipleship (which assumes that if we have done X number of things, we are spiritually mature), we can nevertheless encourage spiritual markers that help young people chart their spiritual progress. Some of these basic markers could include

    a. Scripture memory
    b. Regular Bible reading
    c. Daily devotional times
    d. Completing a discipleship course
    e. Joining the church
    f. Sharing Christ with friends
    g. Service projects
    h. Reading Christian books
    i. Giving a personal testimony
    j. Baptism

2. *Long-term results.* One danger of staying with a youth group only a short time is that we see only short-term results. These can be deceptive. The students who demonstrate the greatest desire for spiritual growth don't always stay with the faith for a long period. Others who seem spiritually dull sometimes return years later as

steadfast believers who want to thank us for everything we taught them—when we had wondered if they were even listening to us.

Neal was a short-term disaster. He never brought his Bible, always disrupted meetings, and seldom seemed interested in spiritual realities. He heard all the facts, but he didn't digest them until his college years. Then, however, he made his commitment to Christ, and the stored facts began to bear fruit: personal growth, zealous Bible study, witness, and sound Christian decisions about marriage, career, and family. Over the long term Neal was a success.

Tina, on the other hand, showed all the signs of spiritual growth in our youth group. She brought her friends to youth activities, read her Bible, and seemed to manifest a genuine love for the Lord. But she never quite got over her love for material possessions. At age twenty, she turned away from the faith. Tina was a long-term failure; but even for her, the final chapter is not complete.

Like the apostle Paul, we will see over the long term that some sow the seed, others water, but God gives the increase. We can work our hardest to present the Christian basics and to stimulate Christian growth, but in the end, God is the one who must, and will, do the ultimate work in their lives.

Resources For Part IV

PERSONAL EVALUATION

Armerding, Hudson T. *Leadership*. Wheaton, Illinois: Tyndale House Publishers, Inc., 1978.

Bustanoby, Andre. *Being a Success At Who You Are*. Grand Rapids: Zondervan Publishing House, 1985.

LePeau, Andrew T. *Paths of Leadership*. Downers Grove, Illinois: InterVarsity Press, 1983.

Raines, Robert. *Success Is a Moving Target*. Waco, Texas: Word Books, 1975.

MINISTRY EVALUATION

Getz, Gene. *The Measure of a Church*. Glendale, California: Regal Books, 1975.

Hauck, Gary. *Is My Church What God Intended It To Be?* Denver, Colorado: Accent, 1979.

Sell, Charles M. *Transition*. Chicago: Moody Press, 1985.

Wiersbe, Daniel, and Wiersbe, Warren. *Making Sense of the Ministry*. Chicago: Moody Press, 1983.

Conclusion: Getting Organized Is a Ministry

Campus Crusade for Christ offers training for their staff leaders in what they call the "Ministry of Management." The title of the training seminar makes a good point: *management is a ministry*. Too often we think of management or administration as a drudgery, a necessary evil of the ministry. Instead, we should realize that management is a ministry, a service offered so that others can grow.

Getting organized is very much a ministry. Planning and administrating our lives, the youth group strategy, and the youth group program is a service that we can offer—not only to the youth but also to the Lord. It is part of the greater process of growth and discipleship, and it shouldn't be shunned as an obstacle to ministry.

With this ministry of management and planning in mind, consider these three statements as a summary of this book.

1. *The basic goal of our ministry should be long-term growth.*

In ourselves and in others, we should be aiming at long-term growth. We are looking to bring others into relationship with Christ and into Christian maturity. This is our ultimate ministry, and our programming and administration is the servant of this goal.

2. *Effective long-term growth that occurs without good organization is exceptional, not normal.*

Jesus may not have had a written program for making disciples, but he definitely had a plan. He knew where he was going and how he would get there. The results in the lives of his disciples were due not only to the spiritual working of the Holy Spirit but also to Jesus' accomplishment of his plan. Good results without good planning comes from good luck, not good management.

3. *Effective long-term growth is facilitated by, not caused by, good organization.*

Again, organization is not an end in itself, but good programs, Bible studies, mission trips, choirs, or the like will be the environments where growth can take place. Making the best use of these growth environments requires careful organization.

Gordon MacDonald, the former pastor of Grace Chapel, was sometimes criticized for his leadership and organization of the Grace Chapel ministry by people who thought the program (or church or sermon or service) was "too professional." As Gordon considered this critique, he would ask, "Well then, what are the alternatives? Shabbiness? Make more mistakes? If we seek excellence, shall we grieve when we achieve it?"

Although we should always be careful to make sure that we aren't trying to be professional as an end in itself, may we aspire to be personally and professionally so well organized that people's only critique is that we are "too excellent." The alternative is undesirable.

Appendix A:
Mission Teams as a Tool for Discipling

How can we disciple our young people? The terms *discipleship* and *youth ministry* are not often linked. Youth ministry is often seen as an intermediate phase, a sort of "holding pattern" in the spiritual growth of a teenager in which we attempt to keep the student out of trouble and in the church until he or she, at age eighteen or beyond, can make intelligent and intense commitments to Jesus Christ.

This vision of youth ministry is unfortunate for two reasons. First, it cheats the youth leaders because it reduces them to baby-sitters or entertainers whose top objective is to keep the teenagers busy. Second, it cheats the students because it concentrates on their immaturity (and tends to perpetuate this immaturity) rather than tapping their vast growth potential.

So how can young people be discipled? How can the youth leader go beyond the "fun-and-games" approach to youth ministry? How can this vast potential for growth be tapped in the teenagers with whom we work?

Many tools are being developed for such discipleship with youth. One option that I favor highly is the idea of a short-term mission project as a tool for discipleship with youth.

My premise is this: *Short-term mission projects, properly executed and led, are the best opportunity in youth ministry for the discipling and development of youth as leaders and as growing people.*

The basis for the premise is ten years of intensive involvement in our youth ministry with short-term summer mission teams. We have sent over fifty teams out on week-long or month-long projects in North and South America, Europe, Africa, and Asia.

Almost all of the projects focused on physical labor (painting is our strength). We have initiated and set up most of the projects through mission agencies, planning the mission project nine or twelve months before the project began. We have recruited one leader for every four students.

To maximize growth in our team members, we ask students to begin praying about involvement as much as eight months before the project. In March, an official presentation of the summer project opportunities are made, and in April we begin to accept applications.

Developing Leadership

The teams must be "properly executed and led." When projects are sloppily executed or led by those who are ill-equipped to work with teenagers, the results can be disastrous. To find those who will effectively lead such teams, look for the leaders with the following qualities and characteristics:

Administrative skill. At least one of the leaders on a team must be a detail person. There will be a myriad of little details (especially on teams that travel overseas), and if these are not cared for, the team will function poorly, and opportunities for discipleship may be lost.

Rapport with teenagers. We have had team leaders who are in their twenties and others who are in their fifties, and both have been successful. The key ingredient is not age but the ability to listen to, understand, and enjoy teenagers. The person who has a great zeal for missions but who has a short temper with those who giggle, talk after "lights out," and turn their noses up at sardine sandwiches will not be effective on a youth team. We have found that the best people to lead youth mission teams are those who have worked with our teenagers throughout the year. The adults who have an established rapport and relationship with the students are more likely to be able to use the intensity of a mission team to the fullest in terms of discipleship.

Spiritual maturity. We can teach others only what we have learned ourselves. If youth mission projects are to maximize the potential of discipling the youth who are involved, the leaders must be established in their own spiritual growth. The key ingredients for which we usually look are consistency in personal devotions, a solid understanding of Christian doctrine, and a commitment to discipling others through relationships and the modeling of Christian lifestyle.

Sense of adventure. A person may be a great administrator, a gifted leader of teenagers, and a man or woman of God, but if he or she will drop dead at the sight of a tarantula, it may be better that he or she not lead the team to South America. The leaders of a mission team need to have the ability to excite the students about the wonderful new things that will be learned on a team experience. If the leaders take on the new experiences as an adventure from God, the students are likely to follow. If, however, the leader is very timid about new experiences, a substantial part of the learning process may be thwarted.

Discipleship Results from Mission Teams

The preparation of both students and leaders for our youth teams has produced more growth in our people than any other aspect of our youth ministry. Leaders have grown out of students who, at first impression, would have been written off as dormant in their spiritual lives. Many parents have commented, "We sent our teens off as immature youth and received them back as growing young adults."

Where has the growth come? In the development of our students, we have seen measurable growth in the following areas:

Personal devotions. The idea of a personal, daily devotional time is familiar to many church youth, but few would claim much success in this area. Two-week projects have enabled us to create a controlled environment where there is a set time each day for this devotional exercise. Students have learned how to make entries in a daily journal (a requirement on many of our teams), and they have experienced a degree of consistency in their prayer life and Bible study. One student commented in an evaluation that the most valuable aspect of his team was that "I got into the habit of either memorizing a verse or having a quiet time every morning." Other students have agreed.

Character development. The intensity of these work projects, the stress, new environments, and the exposure to different cultures has forced students to grow in their endurance, flexibility, and thankfulness. We teach our students the difference between Western values and Christian values by letting them see the fact that not all Christians are the same, look the same, or worship the same. This cross-cultural education has helped students develop their personal priorities. One student stated, "I see how much time I spend shopping; when I saw how poor some people are, I began to rethink my habits. Owning a lot of 'things' just isn't as important to me anymore." Another student, in response to the freedom he experienced on a mission team, came home and sold his television set because "I saw how much time I was wasting watching TV."

Many parents have noticed a new diligence in their teenagers as a result of the mission teams. Many teenagers, especially those under age sixteen, have never experienced a forty-hour work week. When we work on these projects, we work at least that much, and many students are stretched into realizing their own potential as workers.

Personal responsibility. From the outset to the close of the project, students are reminded that they are both a member of a team *and* a person responsible for themselves. Students learn that their behavior directly affects the success of others. If they fulfill their requirements, the team benefits. If they are lazy in their work, the team suffers. Although some would disagree with us, we have allowed students to go off shopping in groups of two or three in foreign countries. Our underlying philosophy has been, "if we treat students as if they are adults and give them responsibility, they are more likely to respond as adults would."

Leadership. Of the students who have served in our mission teams, over half of them have been involved in some sort of leadership in our youth group. As a result of seeing the success of their team on a project, the teenagers have returned with a deeper commitment to serve in the leadership of the youth ministry. The feeling that they have fulfilled their responsibility *there* has led to increased willingness to undertake responsibilities *here*. The positive effect of these service teams has assured students that God wants to use their lives, leading many of them to service in our youth group.

Witness at school. Although we often think that those who want to be missionaries abroad should first be witnesses at home, our youth teams have found that the opposite has also been true: those who have gone out on teams have come back with a new zeal to share Christ with their friends at school. The reasons? Perhaps the deep commitment the project required has given them boldness to witness. Perhaps the exposure to missionaries has given students more understanding of the need to tell others about Christ. Whatever the cause, the effect has been more students who are sharing the love of Christ with others.

The project requirements suggest that team members talk with their peers about what they have learned. This reporting mechanism has taken on various forms. One student did a report in a geology class on "Erosion in the Yukon"; as a result, he was asked why he went and was able to share about the basis for missionary service. Another student produced a slide show for her sociology class based on her mission experience in Newark, New Jersey. As a result, she had an opportunity to share her testimony and was invited to show the production to two other sociology classes!

Servanthood. As a result of these teams, many of our students have learned a deeper sense of what it means to serve others. The work they have accomplished on the teams has been the "behind-the-scenes" variety, and this has taught them the importance of all the ministry work that goes unnoticed and unappreciated. The team emphasis on our projects has taught students how to care for each other. It has been a beautiful experience to watch students care for those who get sick. Through the course of a project, everyone gets an opportunity to serve as an encouragement and support to others.

The lessons of servanthood have been transferred to the home environment as well. Students have learned the importance of serving the members of their own family through the family experience provided by the team. In addition, more students have been willing to take on the obscure tasks in ministry, a factor which we attribute to the mission teams.

Worldwide perspective. Youth workers often are frustrated by the nearsightedness of teenagers, whose crises—whether it be an exam or a new pimple—tend to dominate their thinking. We have been refreshed to find that mission team members have gained a healthier perspective on the world and on their individual lives. Their perspective of God has enlarged as they have seen new lands, new peoples, and new ways to serve God. As a result, the everyday problems they confront have seemed less significant.

This worldwide perspective has led our students to a greater submission to Christ's lordship. Some of our students are headed toward missionary service. Others are not sure but are opening themselves to the call of God. The exciting dimension of this worldwide perspective is that students are becoming more informed about and committed to the work of God throughout the world, and they are starting to see their part in God's worldwide plan.

Appendix B:
Sunday School Curriculum Sources

Accent Publications provides a complete Sunday school curriculum with additional materials for weekday clubs and groups was well as traditional youth meetings and new-convert courses.

Preschool to adults

Accent Publications
P.O. Box 15337
Denver, CO 80215

Bible Way Curriculum is a unified church-school approach, designed to teach basic doctrinal truth to children from grades three to twelve. Parallel material is also available. Of special note, Urban Ministries is a complete curriculum based on the international Sunday school lessons for the whole school.

Age three to adults

Bible Way Curriculum
Education Department
Christian Reformed
   Church
2850 Kalamazoo S.E.
Grand Rapids, MI
   49560

Concordia Publishing House offers a solid, Bible-based curriculum in its *New Life in Christ* series, consisting of a series of study leaflets. Materials include students study guides, teacher's guides, and activity packets.

Preschool through youth

Concordia Publishing
   House
3558 S. Jefferson Ave.
St. Louis, MO 63118

Gospel Light offers non-dated material that provides

Preschool through

Gospel Light
   Curriculum

an opportunity for the youth teacher and student to be creative in learning Bible truths. The packets include all necessary visual aids. A major feature is their "strong commitment to biblical integrity."

Education Division
P.O. Box 3875
Ventura, CA 93006

Gospel Publishing House is an Assemblies of God complete Bible-centered curriculum with teacher's guides, student books, multi-sensory aids including appropriate overhead transparencies.

Preschool through youth

Gospel Publishing House
1445 Booneville Ave.
Springfield, MO 65802

Market Linkage Project for Special Education. Materials available for every possible educational subject and need.

Preschool to high school

LINC Resources, Ind.
1875 Morse Road
Columbus, OH 43229

The Pacesetter Series is a 12 volume[1] set of senior high, topical, youth worker resources. Each includes: background articles by experts, five session outlines, additional bright ideas, a skit or other performance script, and a plan for a retreat or other "out-of-the-church" outing. Each book

Senior high students

David C. Cook
    Publishing Co.
850 N. Grove Ave.
Elgin, IL 60120

---

[1]Volume 1: *Help! Coping With Crisis;* Volume 2: *Inside the Church;* Volume 3: *How Big Is God?;* Volume 4: *Faith Questions;* Volume 5: *Life Choices;* Volume 6: Friends; Volume 7: *Give It Away!;* Volume 8: *The Family;* Volume 9: *The Battle;* Volume 10: *Identity Search;* Volume 11: *The Bible;* Volume 12: *Rites of Passage.*

also provides reproducible student worksheets that coordinate with the sessions.

Randall House Publications publishes a complete line of materials with all necessary visual aids. Their Christ-centered materials are based on the King James Version of the Bible. It is a student-oriented and economical curriculum.

Preschool through adult

Randall House
  Publications, Inc.
Box 17306
Nashville, TN 37217

Scripture Press Publications offers a Bible-centered curriculum. They have Bible studies on a variety of subjects, including personal problems, family problems, and personal needs. Their mission is to promote Christ, inspire Christian living, and teach Bible truth.

Preschool through adult

Scripture Press Publ.,
  Inc.
1825 College Ave.
Wheaton, IL 60187

Standard Publishing makes a complete Sunday school curriculum with all the necessary teacher training materials.

Toddler to adults

Standard Publishing
  Company
8121 Hamilton Ave.
Cincinnati, OH 45231

Resources for Students with Special Needs

The Friendship Series ministers to persons with *mental impairments*. Package includes teacher's manual, group leader's guide, stu-

Youth to adults

The Friendship Series
Education Department
Christian Reformed
  Church
2850 Kalamazoo S.E.

dent resources, multi-sensory kit of slides, posters, flannelgraph, and a videotape introducing the curriculum entitled, "Me, a Teacher?" Teacher trainers are available throughout the country for help in getting started.

Grand Rapids, MI 49560

A resource kit for teaching *deaf* children is published quarterly and includes teaching procedures, evaluation sheet, take-home papers, learning activity, etc.

Beginners to junior high

Sunday School Board of Southern Baptist Convention 127 Ninth Avenue N. Nashville, TN 37234

Sunday school kit for teaching *mentally retarded* persons is synchronized with the curriculum of the Southern Baptist graded series and includes the same aids as the resource kit listed above.

Preschool to high school

Sunday School Board of Southern Baptist Convention 127 Ninth Avenue N. Nashville, TN 37234